PRAISE FOR

"An estimated 43 percent of marriages in the U.S. end in separation or divorce, a grim reminder that most all of us experiences at least one painful breakup in our lifetimes; speaker and certified grief therapist Elliott has come to understand that many aren't successful in overcoming that pain, which can stall anyone's personal and professional life indefinitely. Using her personal experience and stories from her practice, Elliott provides sound advice for those still driving by the ex's house or obsessed with self-blame."—*Publishers Weekly*

"An excellent breakup book that assists not only in dealing with the shock of a relationship ending, but also how to move past the breakup to become a stronger, better person in spite/because of it. Topics such as dealing with breakup myths ("I need closure!") and boundaries (how do I not get into this situation ever again) are refreshing and well-suited to the tone and style. Highly recommended."—About.com

"If you are getting over a failed marriage, or a breakup of a relationship, then this is the must have book that will get you past your pain and suffering. . . . [It] offers hope to those who are suffering. It will show you how to change a life altering experience into something that will change your life for the better."—*Midwest Book Review*

"If you're in recovery from a relationship that ended . . . read this book."—*Kansas City Star*

getting
back
out
there

ALSO BY SUSAN J. ELLIOTT

Getting Past Your Breakup

getting
back
out
there

SECRETS TO SUCCESSFUL DATING *and*
FINDING REAL LOVE AFTER THE BIG BREAKUP

Susan J. Elliott JD, MEd

Da Capo
LIFE
LONG

A Member of the Perseus Books Group

Copyright © 2015 by Susan J. Elliott

All rights reserved. No part of this publication may be reproduced, stored in a retrieval system, or transmitted, in any form or by any means, electronic, mechanical, photocopying, recording, or otherwise, without the prior written permission of the publisher. Printed in the United States of America. For information, address Da Capo Press, 44 Farnsworth Street, 3rd Floor, Boston, MA 02210

Designed by Pauline Brown
Set in 11.75-point Adobe Garamond Pro by the Perseus Books Group

Library of Congress Cataloging-in-Publication Data

Elliott, Susan J.

  Getting back out there : secrets to successful dating and finding true love after the big breakup / by Susan J. Elliott. — First Da Capo Press edition.

    pages cm

  Includes bibliographical references and index.

    ISBN 978-0-7382-1683-6 (paperback) — ISBN 978-0-7382-1684-3 (e-book) 1. Dating (Social customs) 2. Man-woman relationships. 3. Interpersonal relations. 4. Separation (Psychology) 5. Rejection (Psychology) 6. Divorce—Psychological aspects. I. Title.

HQ801.E3977 2014

306.73—dc23

                                                                                              2014031431

First Da Capo Press edition 2014
Published by Da Capo Press
A Member of the Perseus Books Group
www.dacapopress.com

Da Capo Press books are available at special discounts for bulk purchases in the U.S. by corporations, institutions, and other organizations. For more information, please contact the Special Markets Department at the Perseus Books Group, 2300 Chestnut Street, Suite 200, Philadelphia, PA 19103, or call (800) 810-4145, ext. 5000, or e-mail special.markets@perseusbooks.com.

10 9 8 7 6 5 4 3 2 1

In loving memory of
MICHAEL ANTHONY DICARLO
who taught me what real love is

Emotional responsiveness is the basis
of loving and being loved.

—John Bowlby

Acknowledgments

An author needs much support to bring a book to fruition. And when it has been as full of detours as this one has been, it requires much heavier lifting and a stellar supporting cast and crew, and I am blessed with the best one ever.

Deep love and appreciation for the good nature and profound strength of my son Christopher DiCarlo who, as the oldest sibling, knows how to put family first and foremost.

Much love and gratitude to Heather Johnson for her unwavering care and support during the hurricane and my subsequent medical treatment; to Theresa DiCarlo and Marian Erickson for listening and lending support; to my dear friend Candice Cook Simmons whose own remarkable love story is portrayed in these pages.

Much love to my sons Nicholas and Michael and their wives Kristen and Carrie.

Much gratitude for the love and hugs from my beautiful grandchildren, C. J., Derek, Brynn, and Savana. You are my heart.

Much gratitude to my first editor, Katie McHugh, for welcoming the original idea and to my current editor, Renee Sedliar, for Herculean efforts in propelling it forward and listening to me even when I was ranting and raving.

To my St. Helena's/Monsignor Scanlan High School (Bronx, NY) sisters who make up one of the most special groups I've ever been privileged to be a part of. Thank you for your love, support, appreciation, laughter, and care of one another.

For the support and contributions of Julie Hecht, Jane Uitti, Paul Sonkin, Charlene Sanducci Ludwig, and Jamie Flatley.

Enormous gratitude to my doctor, Timothy Mims, for his compassionate care and treatment. Without it, I could not have contemplated this book after suffering so many physical setbacks in such a short time.

To Southside Johnny Lyon for pulling me on stage when I needed it and for the welcoming members of the Jukebox for all the fun at all the shows.

To all my *GPYB* blog and book readers who gave me feedback and answered surveys and shared stories and allowed me to be a part of your process from heartbreak to happiness. You did it!

Contents

Preface

How *Getting Back Out There* Came To Be

When *Getting Past Your Breakup: How to Turn a Devastating Loss into the Best Thing That Ever Happened to You* (*GPYB*) was published in 2009, the preface detailed my personal story of overcoming abuse, getting past a devastating divorce, and building a new life. *GPYB* was written after twenty years of experience doing my own work, working with others, and being happily married to the love of my life, my husband Michael. Two weeks after I submitted the *GPYB* manuscript, Michael was diagnosed with terminal brain cancer. The book was released in April 2009, but my book promotion appearances were limited due to Michael's deteriorating condition.

Fortunately, *GPYB* did well thanks to good reviews, loyal blog readers, and word of mouth. As the book's success grew and I was quoted in mainstream magazines, newspapers, and websites, readers asked if I counseled private clients, especially as they began to work through the *GPYB* relationship, life, and parent inventories and moved back to the world of post-breakup dating and relationships. Readers feeling bereft and lost after their breakup wanted to work with me because *GPYB* discussed breakups within the framework of grieving them as a major loss.

I was, however, dealing with my own loss. After Michael passed in August 2009, my plan was to see my daughter off to college in 2011 and then tend to my own life. I always suggest that readers rebuild after a breakup, and although my situation was different, it was time for me to change my life and move on. My plan fell into disarray when I fell down a flight of stairs and fractured my back. The days and nights that followed, in a large, empty house once filled with laughter and love, seemed endless. After being rocked by my husband's death, I had no idea how much more adversity I would face.

During my recovery process, I developed boot camps and workshops. As soon as I was able, I accepted invitations to speak and to write, as well as appear in local, national, and international media. I consulted for articles, books, and television projects. Helping people heal and build healthy lives gave meaning— once again—to my life.

I started working with a small number of clients getting past a breakup as well as those who had done the work in *GPYB*, rebuilt their lives, and started to date again. I conducted further research on dating and starting new relationships, including surveys and working in small groups. I had an opportunity to speak with people all over the world about their experiences—men and women, young and old, gay and straight, people coming out of long-term relationships, and people emerging from short affairs. Armed with my own experience, my clients' experiences, my friends' experiences, and my research, surveys, and interviews,

I conceived what would become my next book: *Getting Back Out There: Tips for Successful Dating and Finding Real Love After the Big Breakup* (*GBOT*). I had a strict deadline but believed I would finish the book on time.

When It Rains, It Hurricanes

As I worked to clear my calendar and tie up loose ends so I could concentrate on the new book, Superstorm Sandy was getting ready to barrel into New York. I charged my iPod, put new batteries in my headphones, gathered flashlights and candles, and hopped into bed. My bedroom window had a magnificent view of the Hudson River, and storms over the Hudson are an incredible sight.

When the electricity went out, I was propped up on pillows in bed, listening to music and watching the lightning dance along the river. The storm was fierce, and I hoped and prayed everyone was okay. About an hour after the power interruption, a loud alarm began wailing from inside my house. Forgetting that the carbon monoxide detector on the wall gives a signal if it loses power for too long, I assumed the sound was coming from the smoke detector on the living room ceiling and I went to find the ladder. My ceilings are ten feet high, so I had to get up on the top step of the eight-foot ladder to cancel the alarm. I pulled on it, but it wouldn't come loose. Finally I pulled with terrific force and tumbled off the ladder when the detector gave way. As I lay on the wood floor, I knew I was hurt and started crying. "Michael, where are you? I need you now!" The alarm was still going off. Then I looked over to the wall and there was the carbon monoxide detector. I hadn't even needed the ladder.

I went to the hospital and was referred to an orthopedic doctor who said he never saw such an odd break in a hand. I asked for a brace instead of a cast so I could work on my new book. However, the brace aggravated the pain in my hand unless I rested it every hour. I tried to dictate the book, but the transcriptions were a mess. My visits to the doctor revealed that the hand was not healing. I then had a back spasm and injured my knee. When they took an MRI scan of the knee, they found a tumor; 2012 was going from bad to worse. I didn't think, with all my injuries, I would ever complete this book.

I finished moving out of my home in Orange County (New York) to my new home in Westchester County. The day I closed on the Orange County house was right before Christmas 2012. It was a cold and rainy day, but the lightning and thunder on the Hudson held no magic for me. The car was full of the last remnants of my life with Michael, and I cried all the way to my new house. I would never go back to the place where I cared for him for almost a year and where I cradled him in my arms as he passed from this world.

I was a teary mess with a bad back, a broken hand, knee, and heart. On the radio, an advertisement came for Southside Johnny and the Asbury Jukes playing in Ardsley, about fifteen miles from my house. I thought, "If anyone can get me out of my funk, it's Southside Johnny." I was a huge fan, followed the band frequently, and went to many shows in the 1970s and 1980s. In 1986 Southside gave me a harmonica at a Rhode

Island show, and my first husband became so jealous that the tears in the fabric of our marriage became wider. I saw South-side a few more times in the early 1990s but then dropped off the scene, as did he. I had no idea when he came back, but my new life was strange and foreboding and it was time for me to go back to something familiar.

I was feeling homeless, hopeless, and helpless and hoped the show would make me feel connected to something again. It was yet another rainy night in New York when I reluctantly drove to the show. At some point, Southside asked how everyone managed through the hurricane and if anyone had damage. I raised my hand in its cast, and he and I exchanged a few words about it. Later that night he started singing his signature song, "I Don't Want to Go Home," and then—Southside being Southside—pulled me up on stage to sing it with him. The rest of the song is funny and sweet; the video is on YouTube. The next day I went online and found the photos as well as a group of people who followed the band and welcomed me into their circle. I saw many shows in 2013 and always came home feeling energized to write even as my hand was still healing. Finally, a year after it was due, the book was done.

I may have been able to write this book a year ago, but the tumble off the ladder brought me to a new life, which supported me as I did this work and gave me new clarity about the life I had and the life I'm going to have. For all of my readers, I continue to say, as I have before, "Don't give up the day before the miracle happens in your life." This book is the result of my not giving up in mine. I wish you all love and light.

Introduction

This book is the follow-up to *Getting Past Your Breakup: How to Turn a Devastating Loss into the Best Thing That Ever Happened to You* (*GPYB*). While *GPYB* is primarily geared toward healing after a breakup and focusing on the unresolved issues that contributed to your failed relationship, *Getting Back Out There* (*GBOT*) teaches you to avoid the disastrous romances you've had in the past. Getting back out into the dating world after a major breakup takes some work and leaves you with some hard-learned lessons. If you've read *GPYB,* these will be familiar:

1. Breakups are inherently painful, but you can heal if you fully grieve your loss. However, many people shortcut their grief process because it is difficult and they get tired of feeling miserable. They either shut down their feelings or jump into another relationship to repress them, which is why each breakup feels worse than the last. Time does not heal all wounds, and unresolved grief does not go away. Loss piles up into a mountain, making you more afraid to leave a bad relationship, choosing misery over the pain of unresolved grief.

2. Feeling hurt, angry, anxious, upset, and rejected is all part of the grief process. When you return to dating, many of these feelings can resurface and you may think you have "failed" the healing process. You have not. In Chapter 5, these feelings are discussed in detail and you will understand that a certain amount of "recycling" is normal; you can deal with it and learn from it.

3. You must affirm your worth as a person and accept only good things in your life.

4. You must cease contact with your ex no matter what (including passive contact, such as social media stalking), unless you are a co-parent or co-worker, and then your contact should be cordial, minimal, and businesslike.

5. You must review your relationship patterns to see how your last relationship is similar to other relationships and how you have been trying to finish unfinished business with early caregivers.

6. You must develop healthy boundaries and standards. When is "good" not good enough? Have you developed reasonable expectations as to how you are treated in a relationship?

7. You must grasp the concept that love is an action, and what you do is what matters, not what you say.

Central to moving on is coming to terms with the difficult reality that the only thing you can change is you. Knowing that your ex is a drunk, an abuser, a liar, a porn addict, a narcissist, a sociopath, or any number of things may help you become more cognizant and avoid that type now that you are dating again, but you need to stay focused on you. If you don't want to attract someone like your ex, you need to change who you are and refuse to be a victim.

The courageous work of healing old wounds while embarking on a new way of life leads to healthier and happier relationships. At first, there may be things that bear repeating and some things you may not understand completely. The concepts of observation, preparation, and cultivation will be fully explored in this book. While these skills—especially observation—are important when you are recovering from a breakup, they are even more important when you go back to dating and beginning relationships.

The end of *GPYB* includes discussions of the rules of healthy dating, what real love is, and how to keep your standards and boundaries high even when you're madly in love. *GBOT* discusses these in depth; it is a guide for the "new you," helping you make better decisions during the selection process so that you can find real love. It eliminates the guesswork of the past.

GPYB contained a few inventories and were so well-received that I developed new ones for my boot camps, seminars, and workshops and organized them into a workbook. Because readers found them so helpful, I have designed and developed some new ones for *GBOT*. These exercises are designed to help you as you get back out to the dating and relationship world and for you and your new love when you become a couple. Inventories and exercises often help define where you are and where you are going as objectively as possible. Sometimes when you are dealing with emotional issues, the inventories and exercises can ground you in reality. Take advantage of them as much as you can.

While there's no guarantee that you'll immediately fall into the arms of your forever love, most who return to dating after a big breakup benefit from guidance on how to live a healthy life that includes a positive relationship with yourself and strong and lasting relationships with others. The lessons here focus on dating, but you can also use them to make all your relationships healthier, whether with a work colleague, family member, friend, or romantic interest; and to let you know when it's time to put more work into it, when it's fine as it is, and when it's time to walk away.

Not a Typical Dating Book

This is a different kind of dating book. It's not going to give you tips on how to flirt, how to dress, or how to figure out if a person is really interested in you or has an ulterior motive. *GBOT* will touch on some of that, but it focuses on the importance of:

1. Examining your failed relationships for patterns that reveal unfinished business with early caregivers.
2. Keeping your self-esteem high while dating.
3. Observing the world around you so that you can hone and apply your observation skills to any potential lover.

4. Preparing for dating in a new light. If you do what you've always done, you will get what you've always gotten. It's time to prepare for what you want, not just wait around to see what you get.

5. Cultivating your observation and preparation skills so that you see and act on any warning signs ("red flags").

6. Developing your compatibility and standards list of negotiable, nonnegotiable, and possibly negotiable traits that you want in a new love and what to do if you don't find it.

7. Developing and enforcing personal boundaries and reasonable expectations. Unless and until you feel safe, you will not be truly open to another person.

8. Defining and clarifying the parameters of healthy dating.

9. Dealing with "Bumps in the Dating Road: Readiness, Rejection, Recycling, Rebounding, Retreating."

10. Deciding if and when you want to be exclusive with another and asking the right questions before engaging in sexual activity.

11. Examining your early relationship and deciding whether to take it further.

12. If you have children, deciding when and how to introduce your new love to them.

13. Recognizing healthy people and real love. Good relationships that work have common patterns and techniques that like-minded couples employ.

While we all want the next person we meet on a first date to be "the one," it doesn't usually work that way. If you're willing to look at your old relationship patterns and learn new things, chances are you can work your way from getting over heartache to finding someone new who loves you. One client said to me, "I don't know how to find or be in a good relationship." This book is the answer to that dilemma.

Moving Forward

There is nothing as great as the gale-force winds of a new romance to make you forget all you have learned about relationships, abandon the commitments you have made to yourself, and stop building the life you want to have. *GBOT* will keep you grounded and clear about your life while dating and in a new relationship. It is important to maintain focus.

You will learn to observe the new world around you and tune in to people's body language and subtle ways of communicating. Observation is a skill that is important in choosing a mate, but it is disappearing thanks to technology. When everyone is looking down at their phones, no one is paying attention. Learning to observe the world around you is key to observing the person in front of you. When you hone your observation skills, you will be able to pick up hints and clues from others that you may have missed before. After I explained the idea of becoming more cognizant and watching for clues, a client said it sounded like all work and no fun. In reality, observation gives you the freedom to have *more* fun because you now have the tools to work on yourself and handle relationship issues as they crop up. If you're ready to get out there and mingle while considering the idea of falling in love again, you can now do it with confidence.

The Bridge from Bad Relationships to Healthy Love

There is a societal pressure to be partnered. When you are not, you may feel as if the entire world is wondering what is wrong with you. This can strike at any time, but is especially haunting if your friends are engaged, married, or having children. Even though you want what is best for family, friends, and co-workers, the plain truth is that not every relationship is as happy as it appears; some people are settling and not every union is going to last. Although a couple may put on a great facade in public, people close to them may know there are issues in the relationship or that one or both parties are miserable. One man told me about his best friend who seemed to have a nice life with a good wife, a decent home, and two adorable children. But then he stayed with his friend's family for a few weeks while his house was being renovated. Afterward he noted, "They're 'happy' because he gives in to everything she says. If he wants to go out, she vetoes it and tells him his free time is for his family. I was there for six weeks and he met me only once at a sports bar and he lied to her about what he was doing."

When feeling lonely and ready to jump into the dating pool, don't compare your insides to everyone else's outsides. You have no idea what actually goes on between many who seem happily coupled. When you look at your friends and relatives, it is important to note that a healthy relationship makes your life larger and an unhealthy one makes it smaller. Some couples put on a great public face, but there is trouble that others can't see. For the man who could only break away once during his friend's six-week stay, the inability to spend time away from his wife or children has made his life smaller. He has also taken to lying to his wife, which doesn't make him feel good. Additionally, his friends and family have noticed the situation and he feels their pity. Either he will stay miserable or one day he will end things. Right now, there is no way to tell, but the cracks are becoming obvious.

For others, there is dishonesty, jealousy, or suspicion. Some couples fight over major issues such as money or sex while others bicker endlessly over nothing; some spend most of their free time apart because they can't stand being together. Some have porn addictions, and others are forever on the Internet. One man who answered a survey said he sent a cautionary text to his wife while waiting for her to come to bed, "If you bring that phone to bed, we're getting a divorce." Although meant to be humorous, the question "How much texting is too much?" became a daily, monotonous argument that made their home life unhappy. As soon as she picked up her phone, he would roll his eyes and she would clench her jaw. They were at a stalemate and spent many nights in angry silence. There is no way either could have predicted that a thing called "texting," (which didn't exist when they married) would put so much pressure on their marriage that they would cease to enjoy each other's company.

Other couples failed to discuss their viewpoints about standard fare such as the house, children, pets, and other topics that should have been ironed out before they ever mated. A woman told me, "I met Jeff when my boyfriend left me eight months pregnant. He was with me when the baby was born and moved in when I came home from the hospital, treating my son as his own. We married within the year, and I got pregnant again shortly thereafter, thinking a two-year age difference in the children would be perfect. The problem was that he never wanted a second child, content with it being just the three of us. He was so angry at me for not discussing more children, our relationship was never the same and he was never the father to his biological child that he was to my first son." Discussions surrounding what you want out of life are a very important part of coupling. This couple stayed together until the boys were older, but it was never a happy union and Jeff had numerous affairs after his son was born.

After the woman filed for divorce, she blamed her husband for the failure of the marriage, refusing to see her part in it. One thing that people who are successful in relationships have in common is taking responsibility for their part in bad relationships. Otherwise, you are doomed to repeat the same mistakes. Even if you feel you were treated unfairly by your former partner, it is important to look at your part in your former relationship and work on things you can change about yourself.

Despite all the horror stories about relationships gone wrong and the soaring divorce rate, the pressure to be paired leads many to latch on to the first person who seems suitable.

This pressure can cause a person to create a fantasy out of whole cloth that the new person truly fits their "compatible partner scenario," when that is not the case. This happens when people (1) get tired of dating; (2) become convinced this is the best they can do; (3) hear their biological clock ticking or their friends' wedding bells. One woman said, "I knew we weren't going to work out, but I felt like the odd person out as all my friends were turning thirty and getting married. I jumped at the first person willing to put a ring on my finger, though I knew he could be controlling and dismissive. I ignored the number of serious arguments we had and didn't tell even my closest friends how hard it was to get along with him. I didn't want to be thirty-five and not married, so we married when I was thirty-two, had two children, and divorced right before my fortieth birthday. Now I'm forty and divorced with two children that we argue about all the time. Who knows if a better prospect would have come along had I waited? I just didn't want to wait anymore." A milestone birthday such as thirty or forty will push many into the arms of an incompatible mate.

GBOT is about not settling or giving in to pressure that sets you up for failure. You want your next serious relationship to succeed, and you may kiss a few frogs and learn to be comfortable with your alone times on the way to Prince or Princess Charming. Although you may give yourself permission to have some temporary "fun" dalliances in the beginning, as one client put it, "to wash the ex off me," there will come a time when you want to get serious about who you choose to be with and why.

This book will explain how to make sure that you are on the best emotional footing and in the proper mind-set.

How Do I Begin Again?

Suddenly you're in a world where the old ways don't work, but you're unfamiliar with new ones. When uncertain or anxious, people tend to lapse back into their old comfort zones without realizing it. When returning to the dating scene, remember this is new for you in the sense that you've changed since your last relationship. You need to take it slowly, observe what you're doing and why you're doing it. If you become confused, it's okay to take a few steps back or even pull back all the way to reflect on where you're going and how you're getting there. If you've learned to smile again and can be happy without a special someone in your life—"I am me, and I am okay whether alone or partnered"—then you've reached acceptance and integration, which is the other side of loss. Once there, you are ready to go back out into the world and seek out like-minded people who look at life in a healthy way.

After the Breakup: Successful Dating and Finding Real Love

When you return to dating, you may find that you're dealing with life and others in a healthy way. But dating itself may trigger old patterns, doubts, fears, and behaviors. You may become so muddled that you can't remember if you did any work at all.

You wonder if your work was in vain or if you're just the one person in the universe who's never going to get it. Don't worry; the only way not to get this is to choose not to get it. *GBOT* will help you avoid falling into bad habits—or recover easily if you already have.

In almost every relationship you'll find there are bumps in the road, or you may feel that you are being treated badly. The bumps won't rattle you if you're prepared for them and deal with them in a healthy way. It's important to learn the difference between a good relationship with a few bumps, and a bad relationship that lurches from one giant bump to another.

GBOT uses the term "real love" rather than "true love." Readers may have an idealized notion of "true love" from television, songs, and movies. Real love is actual love shown under real life circumstances. Real love is an action expressed between two people who love themselves enough to accept only good treatment from others. When two happy, healthy, and whole souls meet and face life together, magic happens. Yet magic is not what everyday life is made of. Instead, it's wholeness, which carries you through the magical period into the practical, logical, and sometimes painful parts of life.

Life is full of hardships, unforeseen tragedy, loss, and other difficult challenges. Real partners meet those challenges as a team and don't allow outside forces to tear the fabric of their love. Instead, they rise up as one to meet difficulties while being supportive, giving, and understanding. Real partners want what is best for their lives, individually and collectively. The members of a team may have separate interests, hobbies, and friends, but when hard times happen, the team cannot be divided. That is what real love looks like, and it is richer and better than any starry-eyed gaze over a glass of champagne. The "real" in "real love" is about real life and everyday foibles, trials, triumphs, and tribulations. You are real by yourself and real with each other, and you tackle real life in a real way. That is real love, and this book explains how to find it.

chapter 1

The Steps from the Big Breakup to Happy and Healthy Dating, Mating, and Relating

After a breakup, you are challenged to rebuild your life while learning to value yourself as a single person. Perhaps you were rejected by someone you truly cared for, or your relationship simply didn't work. You may now be considering some kind of foray back into the world of dating. Being ready doesn't necessarily mean being fully recovered from what happened to you in former relationships or in childhood. A client lamented, "If I wait until I feel like I've worked through my stuff, I won't be dating for another ten years!" Have no fear; you don't have to wait ten years. I'm simply reminding you that just because you may feel ready to get "back out there" doesn't mean all the work is done. Vigilance will help you balance a continued learning experience while greeting new people and situations.

There's probably no way to stay out of a relationship until you've worked through issues that may have contributed to problematic relationships. However, you have to keep working as an individual, and perhaps as a couple, once you find a good mate. This isn't meant to sound gloomy or imply that everything is work; it's just something to keep in mind as you go through this stage of your life. Remember that you're still learning even though it's tempting to yell, "Yippee! I know what I'm doing! Look out world, here I come!"

For some of you, the breakup was a brief pit stop, and you'll continue along your way and find better partners. Others may have ended a relationship with someone who was truly disturbed, had a personality disorder, or was abusive. No matter where you come from, you have to remember what you've learned to be truly successful in finding a wonderful partner and creating a great relationship next time around. If you did come out of a relationship with someone who had deep issues and complex problems, your recovery may take longer, but you'll get there if you understand that just because the individual is gone does not mean the problem is gone. Whether or not your own dysfunctional past and unfinished business led you into this relationship or you were an unwitting victim of a disturbed individual, you have to examine your reasons for getting in and for staying. It may be as simple as you "didn't know that you didn't know" or complex in a way that it represented your need to win over a long-ago struggle with an unloving caregiver or unresolved childhood trauma.

Too many come out of a bad breakup looking for "the one" when what they really need is time to work on themselves, figure out what qualities they want in a suitable partner, and date a few people who are "not the one" before they're ready for something permanent. Almost every person I work with can post an online dating profile seeking honesty and walks in the moonlight, but few make a list of standards and boundaries that gets down to the nitty-gritty of what they value in another person. Sometimes you need to "date around" before your list is complete and you know what you're looking for in a mate. You may think that you're ready to find your forever love (and you may be); or you may need to date for a while, pull back, and then go back out; or you may need to continue to work on your issues and your list while you date casually.

A client recently shuffled into my office, flopped onto the couch, and buried her head in a pillow. "Tom and I are no longer dating! Another failure! Back to the drawing board! I hate this." I let her vent for a while and then gently reminded her that "back to the drawing board" doesn't mean failure; it means continued learning for the best possible outcome. Granted, you don't want that answer, but once you learn to not take a breakup so personally or put so much stock into the first few dates, you become dedicated to finding the most compatible mate, not just avoiding another false start.

Another client kept her dedication strong when she realized that she had been through so many things with unworthy people that the only way to make those experiences meaningful was to use them as the impetus to get it right. By reframing her approach to dating as a chance to learn something rather than becoming hopeful and excited to find the love of her life, she was able to be more relaxed with new men. By being less hesitant and less intense, she was more attractive to others and less likely to fault herself when things didn't work out. When she put her commitment to herself first and then did her best to have a good time no matter how likely or unlikely a partnership would be, higher-quality people came into her life. Once she decided to do the choosing instead of waiting to be picked, her sense of control led to a new confidence that attracted healthier people.

One client had been practicing what you will learn as "tuck it in your pocket" observation. She started a conversation with a man online, who canceled the first two dates they planned. She was unsure what two cancellations represented, so she tucked this observation into her mental back pocket. The third time he gave her very detailed directions to the meeting place. Later he remembered a part of the route that might seem confusing, and he texted her to bear left at this place. She observed to herself that going over the directions he gave her was "thoughtful," but again did not know what it really meant so she tucked it away. The "tucking" is akin to assembling a jigsaw puzzle. You pick up a piece and think you know where it fits, but it doesn't fit anywhere so you put it to the side and wait until you have filled in more pieces so now it becomes obvious where it belongs.

They met and enjoyed themselves; sometimes he seemed fully engaged and other times detached. This back-and-forth between someone who cared about where he was and someone who didn't approximated the way she had been seeing him prior to the date.

He politely paid for the dinner and walked her to her car. As they parted ways, she had a feeling, later confirmed when she never heard from him again, that he wasn't enthralled by her. Instead of looking for what was wrong in herself, she thought about the two times he canceled and now the puzzle was becoming clear: he was "flaky." As someone who had overlooked too much before, this realization was a true triumph for her. She did not feel rejected by him as she recognized that his running hot and cold was not what she needed. As pleasant as the date was, she dismissed him when she realized that he wasn't going to contact her again. That is an example of taking your self-esteem to a level higher than someone else's opinion of you, and it is crucial to successful dating.

At some point you need to take time to change or enhance your life—whether it's through *GPYB*, traditional therapy, employing Eastern philosophies such as mindfulness and meditation, twelve-step programs, reading self-help books, or all of the above. Recognize that your post-breakup time is a journey of self-discovery that can take awhile, even years. This doesn't mean you can't date for ten years, but that you have to continue your self-discovery work even after you get into a new relationship. Don't throw away the new you for a new relationship. The trade-off is not worth it.

Take Your Time and Don't Forget the Work You've Done

Once you have made a strong commitment to yourself and have moved past thinking about your ex, you can focus on the real compatibility of a new love interest. *Does this person like me?* You want someone who sees your value and understands that you are a special person. If you are not getting that feedback early on, it's time to move on. Once it's clear that someone does like you, the next question is, *Is this someone I can make a life with?* That can't be answered early or easily, but keep it in mind as you explore a new relationship.

If you've been entrenched in one or more dysfunctional relationships, emotional health may be something you are still working on and you are unsure about how to "pick" right. Truth be told, more unhealthy people are available than healthy ones, but the more you care for yourself and do the things you need to do, emotionally healthy people will come into your life. Some days may seem like you're looking for a needle in a haystack, but it's important to stay the course and reject unsuitable suitors.

The good news is that there are people out there who are naturally easygoing and fun. There are those who have triumphed over adversity; some have worked through their issues and understand that creating lasting, real love takes two special, determined people. The "good" people, whether they are that way because it's their nature or because they've worked through things, are going to treat you with love, kindness, understanding, honesty, and a dedication to making a good thing better. They are out there, so don't settle for less. Remember: you get what you put up with. From now on, you will accept only the best.

This book is designed to help you form a healthy relationship when you find the right partner. It's meant to be a guide for everyone, but some will read this chapter and think, "This has nothing to do with me. My childhood was great, my ex-partners aren't bad people and all this 'working through' is a bunch of nonsense." I want to stress that this book is not entirely about that. Although this book will talk in length about red flags—warning signs that should give you pause—it will also talk about "pink flags" that might raise a concern. If you haven't been severely damaged in the past or if the issues your partner showed in the beginning were more pink flags than red ones, you can still use this book. It will show you, no matter what kind of background you come from, or how loved or unloved you were, how to be a better "partner picker."

Not everyone is walking around as a pile of neurotic behaviors waiting for a compatible pile of neurotic behaviors for a relationship. Many find themselves in failed relationships because they haven't looked at their problems closely enough to resolve them or haven't taken the time to make a compatibility and standards list or to observe those they choose. Some people have small issues that have kept them in failed relationships and others have bigger ones. This book will show you the best possible ways to address any issue, big or small, and find answers to age-old questions: Is it me? Is it my partner? Is it us? Coming out of relationships, most people don't know the answers, and this book will help you find them before you get ready to make a commitment to someone.

Each relationship has a different ending, and therefore each beginning will be different too. You may think you're ready to date as soon as the ink is dry on the divorce decree (or even sooner), or because it's been over a year, or because your ex found someone new. You may think you're ready because you're bored, lonely, and want someone to find you attractive. However, there's almost no way to tell, for certain, that you're ready, when you'll wake up and yell, "This is it! This is the day I'm fully 'cooked' and ready, willing, and able to take on the world of 'finding a new love.' I'll be all right no matter what happens." That realization isn't going to come in a flash. But it should come after you've developed a relaxing, inner knowing voice. This is also when you realize that you can size up anyone you meet, commit to leaving when red flags become too ominous or too numerous, and learn to be okay no matter what. Once you know that, you can find a successful relationship with the right person.

There's no secret formula and everyone is different, but if you follow the guidelines here, you'll have the confidence and self-worth that healthy people are drawn to. Abusers, alcoholics, sociopaths, psychopaths, and narcissists are looking for victims. Equally undesirable are the cheaters, the cheapskates, the manipulators, and the passive-aggressive. If you think about your relationships, you most likely can add a few more to the list, such as those who are not ready for a committed relationship or those enmeshed with family or ex-partners. If you refuse to present yourself to the world as a victim lacking boundaries or standards, you will never have to deal with these types again. You can simply be yourself and other healthy people will appear. Build your life, follow your dreams, forget about the opinions of others, and don't place unfair expectations on yourself. You'll not only have fun dating, but you'll also learn to be choosy and secure about your forever mate when you find him or her.

GBOT will introduce five important questions to ask and answer while dating. After a breakup, many fear they will never be comfortable again or will never find someone to love. By using these important tools, you will feel comfortable on your journey to finding someone to love who will love you for who you are and value you as a person and a partner. Real love does exist, and you will find it if you follow these tried and true paths.

chapter 2

Are You Ready?
Five Questions to Ask
Before You Take the Plunge

Carin, 28 / I am glad I took the time between grieving my old relationship and starting to date to learn to "people watch" because I did learn to pick up subtle clues and read people better once I was out in the dating world. I'm surprised at how vigilant I became and how much it helped.

Sara, 31 / I had a very difficult time doing the life inventory and comparing my relationships to my unfinished business with my parents, but it wasn't until I got honest about that, did things start to change for the better.

Loren, 44 / One thing I learned was that I was treating dates like job interviews. There was a job I desperately wanted (to be the lifetime love of this perfect person) without even knowing if this was a perfect person or someone I wanted to be involved with longer than one dinner date.

Joanna, 35 / When I broke up my relationship, people kept telling me to "get back out there," but I wasn't ready and couldn't figure out how to be ready. The most helpful thing was telling myself over and over that I would be okay no matter what and until I felt that, to the depth of my being, I wasn't prepared for what can be a really rough ride.

There are five main questions to ask yourself before you go back to the dating scene, and we will explore them in depth. Chapter 2 concentrates on questions 1, 2, and 3, and Chapter 3 on questions 5 and 6.

The Five Questions of Getting Ready for Healthy Relationships

Until now, the refrain has been, *Keep the focus on you.* But now it is time to switch gears. Yes, after all those reminders to stop thinking about the ex and the constant reminder that what "everyone else thinks of you is none of your business," we're going to head in another direction. We're going to put the focus on others in a well-guided, healthy way that will help you avoid romantic minefields and miserable relationships. Ask yourself these five important questions before going back out there after the big breakup:

1. Have I looked closely enough at my past relationships to recognize patterns and behaviors that need to change?
2. Is my self-esteem strong enough to face and withstand judgment and rejection?
3. Have I learned to truly observe myself and others in an objective way to take note of red flags and warning signs?
4. Am I prepared to return to dating with a new mindset to cultivate loving relationships?
5. Will I remain true to my boundaries and standards even as I become swept up in falling in love again?

Relationship Patterns and Life Inventory

Question 1: Have I looked closely enough at my past relationships to recognize behavior patterns that need to change?

The most important thing to do before going back out there is to look at and learn from your relationship patterns, using the life inventory. If you've already done the *GPYB* life inventory, you can refer to it. If you have not done the inventory, you will find it on page 19 in this book. The life inventory asks how your early development and teenage years affected your adult relationships. Some will say, "They haven't," while others will think about it; a few will know exactly where the influence is coming from. A majority of people understand that their past may have something to do with the bad partners they've picked but not exactly what. The first step to successful dating and relationships is to know what you were trying and failing to achieve in your former relationships. To do that, you must go back over all your familial, friendly, and romantic relationships. A new beginning is a great motivator to examine the past, and that is why *GBOT* continues the self-examination from *GPYB*.

Everyone forms relationship patterns early in life. Your patterns may stem from a difficult childhood or a few bad experiences in early relationships. Babies form attachments to their caregivers, and attachment issues can arise that lead to bad relationships later in life if the caregivers fail to be nurturing and present. Though people do not remember their earliest interactions with their parents, they can usually guess, later on, if they were securely attached or not. Often a major breakup will lead people to examine their attachment patterns and fix them before trying new attachments. Pain motivates people to look into places they've tried to avoid.

Many people come from homes where one or both parents were absent or ambivalent toward them. Subsequently they have formed relationships with people who are withholding or ambivalent. By choosing unavailable partners, they are trying to gain the attention of the uninterested parent.

I offer one of my most telling examples of this to serve as a model you can use to examine your own relationships. A client came to see me after a series of failed relationships. When we looked at the patterns in her relationships, we noticed that all of the men she was involved with were unloving and ambivalent toward her. Instead of walking away from those relationships, she ran after the men, hoping to change their minds and get their attention. By "ran after" I mean literally. One man walked away from her after announcing he did not want to be involved any longer, and she ran after him in the pouring rain and then slipped and fell in the street. He glanced back to see what happened, waited for her to get up, and then continued on to his car. She chased him until he pulled away, leaving her standing in the rain, bleeding and hurt from her fall. How had she come to think so little of herself that she allowed such bad treatment? How had she come to a place in her life where she would chase someone through the rain who clearly was not interested in her?

We looked at her relationship with her parents and discovered they had a very different relationship with their older children than with her. She had to dig into her past to find out what was "wrong" with her, and her previous therapist encouraged her to talk to her older siblings and try to find out how their childhood differed from hers. I concurred that something was "off" and she needed to find out what it was. What happened?

Her three much older siblings described the parents who raised them as warm, nurturing, and closely involved in their lives. As adults the three had securely attached, loving relationships with interested and caring partners, while my client had terrible relationships, each one making her feel more unlovable than the last. She felt rejected and unloved by her parents and concluded that they did not want a child later in life but she just "came along." All of her relationships reflected this belief. She became involved with men who really didn't want a relationship but took up with her as she "came along." Trying to win her parents' love and approval, she chose to work straight out of high school instead of going to college, as her siblings had done. She lived at home, putting in much overtime, so she could buy her parents elaborate gifts and send them on expensive trips. She showered her parents with gifts to buy their love. Yet they remained detached from her.

Her relationships with cold, distant men mimicked the patterns of her relationship with her parents. To start on the road to healthy relationships, it was necessary for her to look at her siblings' trajectory to happy marriages and find out why she was different. The investigation revealed a family secret that no one talked about and yet explained everything.

When the three children were in junior high, they became increasingly involved with friends and activities. The parents felt lonely and decided to have more children. They had a son and two years later, my client. Shortly after she was born, her mother sat on a park bench feeding her and watching her toddler son who ran and fell down, hitting his head hard on the pavement. He cried a little but seemed okay. Her oldest child was a son who used to run and fall, as boys do, so the mother thought nothing of it and took the two children home. Later that night the boy died in his sleep of traumatic brain injury, something that was not understood at the time. The mother, bereft with grief and guilt, could barely take care of the baby. The once warm family fell apart and, as the older children moved out, the father distanced himself from his wife and child. Even though the boy's death had blown the family apart, there were no photos of him in the house, and he was never acknowledged or discussed. In high school and then in college, and glad to be away, the older children rarely visited the home that was now unrecognizable to them and failed to create a relationship with their sister.

My client grew up with a depressed mother who never received treatment and sat on the couch in a dark house with the curtains drawn tightly against the outside world. Her father was distant, almost as if he was afraid to love her. As a result, she did not form the secure attachment her siblings had, did not see her siblings much, and assumed it meant there was something wrong with her and, as a result, sought out people like her parents who were incapable of fully committing or attaching to her.

My client's early life with parents who would not or could not attach to her led to many bad relationships. Her quest was to find a person who would love her as she always needed to be loved, but she was attracted to those she was comfortable with— detached and incapable partners. She had to look at her relationship patterns and see that she was trying to make emotionally unavailable people love her, thereby "winning" the struggle with her parents. She used affirmations and positive self-talk to change her view of herself as unlovable and to commit that she would partner only with those who wanted to be with her. She had to observe, prepare, and cultivate a different mind-set smart, and sweet. A guy on a date with her who didn't follow up for a second had something wrong with him, not her. I had to keep reminding her so she could keep reminding herself, "It's only one date." If you're imagining forever scenarios over the first cup of coffee, slow down. It's only one date. Say that every time you have a great first date.

Many have fallen prey to sociopaths because they had no idea how charming and convincing sociopaths can be. If you were brought up well-to-do with others who were also well-off, you may not be aware of people who want to use you for your money. You see the world as you are and base it on your own frame of reference—how you were raised. If you are trustworthy and reliable, you may think everyone is that way. That kind of naïveté can lead you to bad relationships. It's time to learn new things about the bad people of the world and to arm yourself against them.

The Life Inventory

If you have done the *GPYB* life inventory, review your work before embarking on a date. If you have not, the inventory is as follows:

1. On a piece of paper, write "Positive" on one side and "Negative" on the other.
2. Review your most recent relationship and write all the positive aspects of your former partner and then all the negative ones in the appropriate columns.

3. Think through all of your attachments in life—romantic (involved or just a crush) or familial or friendly. Write down the negative and positive attributes of each one.

4. Look over the list you've made and write down similarities and patterns among the people included.

5. Take another piece of paper and make a list of positive and negative traits for your parents or earliest caregivers.

6. Review your lists and see which of your exes, friends, or family members have similar traits. Write the positive traits on one piece of paper and the negative ones on the other.

7. Which similar traits have been most destructive in your life? Which have been most helpful?

This part of the inventory will take some time. Don't rush through it. You can continue to uncover your past and all the various connections as you move ahead into the dating world. Look at your lists of negative traits. What are you trying to achieve by seeking out each destructive trait? For example, if you find "abandoned me" appearing on your lists, it means that you are picking people who have abandoned you and the question is, Are you trying to win over an abandoning parent? You may see "critical" describing many on your list, including your father. The question is, Are you trying to win approval from a critical parent?

Take your time, days or even weeks, to complete this exercise. Concentrate on the negative traits that have influenced your choices and your ability to sustain a relationship. The unfinished business you have been trying to resolve is where your comfort zones are. To date happy and healthy people, you must change your comfort zones and your inner messages.

Once you have finalized your inventory, leave it for a while and center yourself again. After several days, come back to the list and pick out the most important items. Look at the relationships that have been most damaging, including your parents and siblings. With each relationship, identify the most hurtful elements. Over the course of a few weeks, write a letter (that you do not send) to these people including all the things you want to say. Pretend you are having a conversation and write full sentences. End your letter with, "I release the power you have had over me and reclaim who I am meant to be."

When you are ready, ask a friend or therapist to listen to your letter or letters. When you are finished reading, talk about how you felt as you worked on this exercise or how you feel now. You may feel many things; it's not important to identify them all. On the other hand, you may feel nothing or sheer exhaustion. Whatever you feel, it's okay. It's your process and you can feel whatever you feel.

Later burn the letter and say aloud, "Thank you for the time spent in my life, but now I let you go with love." Even if you're angry and don't feel love, saying it this way precludes anger or spite. Letting someone go with love is for your benefit, not theirs.

After you have finished your life inventory and identified your relationship patterns, it is time to give back to yourself.

Look at your inventory as a guide to what is missing in you and what you need to give to yourself in terms of confidence and self-esteem. You can achieve this with affirmations and self-care, confirming that you are a wonderful person deserving of all good things. When you have positive accolades as the center of your self-worth, positive people will come into your life. Once you gain a firm footing and you incorporate the next four parts into your dating, you're ready to go!

Affirmations

Question 2: Is my self-esteem strong enough to face and withstand judgment and rejection?

Dating involves judging and being judged and often leads those with low self-esteem or low self-worth to pick the wrong people. If you are among those who have recently raised their self-esteem, you may need to develop new affirmations for dating.

An affirmation is a brief and present statement that gives you positive feedback about yourself. A short one that I recommend to all my clients is, "I am okay no matter what." A longer one might be, "I am a good, loving, confident, and cheerful person who succeeds at challenging tasks." During dating you may find yourself rejected by some who, you feel, should be lucky to have you. This can lead to self-doubt. Your affirmations are the place to turn to first. You say, "[Name of person rejecting you] is an unsuitable mate. I want to be with people who want to be with me." Repeating the second part of that affirmation is crucial to keeping high self-esteem during the dating process. Although you may want to look at patterns that aren't working for you and haven't worked for you, first revisit any setback to your self-esteem that a negative encounter may have caused.

If you have been pursuing critical people to win over a critical father, you develop an affirmation that says, "I approve of what I do. I am with people who approve of me from the start. I ban negative, critical people from my life." You can work on your affirmations and develop ones that speak to you and help you to be what you want to be. If you have been with abusive people you can affirm, "I demand love and respect from those in my life." If you have been with blaming partners, friends, or co-workers—those who seek to make you the person who is always wrong—you can affirm, "I take responsibility for my words and actions and expect others to do the same."

Affirmations are integral to keeping your self-esteem high and are very powerful when written correctly and used every day. Many people try to avoid affirmations. Some are immediately turned off by the term, "affirmation," or say they don't understand what they are, or think they are silly or "new agey and Oprah-esque." I have worked with clients for over twenty years and can say, without a doubt, affirmations work when written correctly and used every day.

A few things to know about affirmations:

- Affirmations are not "new-agey" but are based on science.
- Affirmations are designed to cause some discomfort so that you can expand your comfort zones.

- If you don't build a foundation with affirmations, the rest of your healing work, and ultimately your success, will suffer.
- Keep tweaking your affirmations but don't keep changing them.
- Affirmations take at least thirty days to work and a core group of ten to fifteen should be said every day, several times a day.

When you have negative situations and people in your life, you come to define yourself by their standards. Positive affirmations replace the negative messages you've been given. They will *change* your self-image and *empower* you to become a better and stronger person who demands and receives loving treatment from others.

The key to effective affirmations is to do them right and often. Have at least ten affirmations that you say twice a day while you are at rest. It takes thirty days for a new affirmation to begin to imprint on your subconscious; therefore, be sure to do your affirmations in a systematic way for at least thirty days.

A negative self-image may be so ingrained that saying and believing even brief affirmations is difficult. However, you need to start somewhere, so it's okay to start small. When working with affirmations, you are working with your subconscious, which forms your skills, habits, tendencies, and self-image. Your subconscious feeds you information about who you think you are, and your subconscious can only work with the information it has. If you receive negative messages from yourself and others, your self-image will be negative. When working with the sub-conscious, there is good news and bad news:

1. The *bad news* is that the subconscious is highly im-pressionable, and that is why entertaining the same negative thoughts all the time is so easy. If, in early childhood, you were given negative feedback about yourself, you still believe it because your subconscious has not been told anything different. You are stuck repeating the same negative patterns, actions, and responses because you have been *programmed* to do so via your subconscious. Think back to my client who was the youngest of her siblings. Because her siblings received good and loving treatment, they had good and loving partners, but once the family secret was revealed, it became clear that her parents' behavior toward her had nothing to do with her.

2. The *good news* is that you can change your subcon-scious thoughts with positive messages, to "re-ingrain" it the way you want it to be. Affirmations work be-cause your subconscious believes what you tell it, so long as you tell it often enough in a way it under-stands. You can re-ingrain or retrain your subcon-scious by feeding it consistently positive messages. My client with the grieving, unhealed parents af-firmed that she was lovable and deserved love and loving, attentive people in her life and that is what came into her life. It was hard work and required

many hours of journaling and writing affirmations, but being in bad relationships is much harder and she was able to put that behind.

Your subconscious has a lot of responsibility, but it is very basic and simple:

- It understands only discrete, easy concepts.
- It takes statements literally.
- It doesn't know the difference between reality and the power of suggestion.
- It knows only the present.
- It does not understand negative phrasing or anything that is not present.
- It responds well to visualization.

Understanding your subconscious will affect the way you write affirmations and make a big difference in the degree of success you have with them. When Henry Ford said, "Whether you think you can or you can't, you're right," he was referring to the subconscious mind.

Saying "I can do this" or "I can do [whatever it is you want to do]" is a fundamental affirmation that you need to repeat until it is ingrained in your subconscious. These basic affirmations are the mantra of successful people. They believe they can *do* it. Even if they fail at first, they will keep going and find another way to go about *doing* it. It never occurs to them that they can't do it. Because when you believe you can, you will find a way to do it or to try a new path that is more suitable and successful.

Develop affirmations that affirm your worth to the world. When feeling rejected or unloved, many women affirm, "I am a woman of grace and dignity and I deserve a partner who appreciates that." Many men affirm, "I am a man of honor and integrity and I deserve a partner who appreciates that." You can change the wording to fit what speaks to you, but it's important to have your affirmations at the ready if you are dating again. Feeling rejected by someone you like can be devastating, even someone you hardly know. Replace your negative thoughts and feelings *immediately* with positive affirmations. Do not allow yourself to wallow or reflect the rejection back to you. Do not let someone's bad feelings about you fester.

Many who engage in online dating find that they open up easily via text or email only to be shut down in person or find someone they like moving away without explanation. The feelings associated with rejection, such as, "I'm not worthy," must be counteracted with strong and powerful affirmations. You did not come all this way from your last breakup to feel worthless, which really is just a reflex reaction to a disinterested person or a bad first date. Use your affirmations to combat those feelings.

Acceptance Statements

Another type of affirmation helpful for dating is acceptance statements. If there are things that confuse, puzzle, anger, or keep you stuck, you need to move past them and get on with life. Obsessing over things, searching for answers you're never going to find, does no good. In a search for peace, people try to find the right words to convince someone to stay or that they make a good couple. Many live in a fantasy world instead of accepting things as they are.

Other times people have residual anger from the past and need to accept and let go of those circumstances. If you have issues with accepting present or past situations or if anger at something or someone has negatively impacted your life, you need to write acceptance statements to clear your side of the street. If you can develop five to ten acceptance statements about things that are driving you crazy, you will find this helpful when you're dating and you really like someone who appears to be rejecting you for whatever reason. You can say, "I accept that X has different plans for her life that I fail to fit into." If you feel angry at your ex for really ending the relationship you can say, "I accept that my ex is never coming back and my life is better off without someone who doesn't want to be with me."

Finally, try to visualize yourself in your desired situation. You can imagine yourself holding hands with a lover in front of a fireplace or going for a walk. Visualize someone telling you how beautiful or handsome you are. Take time to close your eyes and visualize your affirmations coming true. A client of mine was ready to embark on a European trip with her law school class-mates, most of whom were younger than she. Weeks before the trip she regretted her decision to go, feeling shy and awkward. We worked on affirmations and visualizations that boosted her confidence and friendliness. We spoke frequently throughout her trip, and she was having a wonderful time with her class-mates and the new people she was meeting. Whenever her old self-doubt crept in, we worked on increasing the frequency of some of the affirmations. Now she recounts it as "the trip of a lifetime." You can have the same success in relationships when you affirm and visualize your affirmations coming true. Remember: you can do this!

Observation

Question 3: Have I learned to truly observe myself and others in an objective way to take note of red flags and warning signs?

Dating requires keen observation of others and sure self-awareness. Many failed relationships start with a heady enthusiasm that affects your ability to sit back and assess your new lover clearly or causes you to ignore red flags or hints about what issues you may encounter later. Although you may date some losers, get into some semiserious relationships, and have your heart broken another time or two, don't be discouraged. See nonsuccesses as contributions to your awareness of what's good and what's not so good. See nonsuccesses as opportunities to refine your idea of an ideal mate and know that the more knowledge you have of what you truly want and need, the better your chances of finding the one real love that will last forever.

During your breakup recovery, you learned to step back and observe yourself in different situations and with different people. Now you are going to take your observation skills and apply them to the outside world. You will prepare to interact with others and cultivate healthy behavior whether you're in a relationship or not. As you have done with yourself, you will learn to see things in other people that you would have missed before. You will become a keen observer of others to fill your life with happy, healthy people. It is now time to balance the focus on you with the focus on others.

There are two important components of dating successfully and forming good relationships. The first is to know who you are and the second is to know who others are, not who they purport to be. "Knowing others" means picking up subtle clues and hints and not being surprised if people act strangely months later. I work with clients on red flags and the hints and clues that things were not going to go well from the beginning. Many times you see them but don't know what to do with them. Do they reveal a fatal flaw such as infidelity or a subtle flaw you might be able to learn to live with? When finding someone who is fun or very attractive, it's easy to miss the signals that imply a long-term relationship may be a disaster. If you see them, you may have to act on them and boot the fun person from your life, and part of you may rebel against that idea. You've been so lonely for so long, you don't want to acknowledge a few red flags that might mean nothing at all! However, ignoring them has gotten you into trouble in the past. No matter how much fun someone is, or how much attention you're receiving, the side that "knows better" needs to take a closer look at what is going on with your fun person.

Although it's work, observing others is akin to developing a sixth sense. When you hone the invaluable skill of observation, you feel safe because you can trust your own instincts. The ability to read others, or to see past a person's facade, is what makes those red flags appear bright and undeniable. Even when dealing with master misery artists such as passive-aggressive personali-ties, narcissists, or sociopaths, the truth about them becomes clear when you know what you are looking for and are healthy enough to recognize it. Nevertheless, before you can change your responses and behaviors, you must get a sense of the full picture—through observation.

Observing Others in an Objective Way

As a group facilitator in the corporate world in the 1990s and then in my own early counseling practice, I taught students and clients to become keen observers *of* their own lives and *in* their own lives. Amazingly, people participating in a workshop designed to help with attentiveness found creative ways to avoid paying attention! While I talked to the group about becoming more observant, at least one person would be doodling on a pad and another looking out the window. Even when people seek information about how to be present in their own lives, they have such ingrained habits of inattention that they scribble even while trying to hear what they need to do to increase their attentiveness!

This jaunt down memory lane is to remind you that today's technology is not completely responsible for people "zoning out." However, the overuse of technology has definitely made the problem worse and makes it more difficult to step back and evaluate a situation you're in because you forget to take time out to think about it and analyze it. Even before everyone spent all day staring at their smartphones, I'd tell my students and clients to put away the distractions, go out to a public place, and become aware of the people around them—their body language and the way they're looking at you and talking to you or others.

"Tuck It in Your Pocket" Observation

When starting to observe, you may have no idea what to do with the observation. Sometimes people do things that we may question or find objectionable. For those who spent years excusing other people's bad behavior, it's almost second nature to do so. But it's now time to make everyone who comes into your life accountable. When you start dating again, you will not always know what an action says about a person until you have been out a few times. Occasionally something will bother you on a first date, but not so much that you are ready to end it; you may have to wait and see if this is just an anomaly you happened to see on an "off" night.

A woman met a man during a trip abroad and spent much platonic time with him; he seemed nice, friendly but not too forward. He was handsome, a great conversationalist, and was moving to her city in the next year. He asked if he could take her out when he got there. The first time, he asked her to pick a place because he didn't know the city. She did and met him there. When the date was over, he said good-bye as he walked one way down the street, and she the other. He did not offer to put her in a cab, and she asked me what I thought. I said, "See what happens the second date." Again, he had her pick the place and again he had her find her own way home. On the third date, he picked the place, seemed very interested in getting physical, and was suddenly very interested in how she got home because he wanted to go there too. This rude, self-centered behavior was who he was, but it didn't become clear until the second date and then was confirmed on the third.

You don't always need to go to a third date, but considering the conflicting information she had about him from the trip and then how he acted when he arrived in her hometown, she gave him a few chances. When met with the evidence of who he was, she could choose to lower her standards and accept the rude behavior or move on. She moved on.

This is "tuck it in your pocket" observation. You can't always tell if someone is being self-centered, rude, obnoxious, or moody from just one encounter or a single date. However, you can't ignore it either. There comes a point where you have to take the information out of your back pocket, look at it, and make a decision. *Does this action say who this person really is? If so, is this someone you want?* Don't let other factors interfere with this. If someone stands you up, blows you off, or mistreats you in the beginning, the chances are high that it's going to happen again. You don't have to tuck such obvious behavior into your back pocket. But a guy who doesn't know his way around the city may lean more heavily on you than a guy who does. He may be absent-minded and leave you standing by yourself, but once he settles down, you need to raise your expectations. If this behavior continues, then he's not just confused and new. Observation is a matter of timing. You're able to see if someone is truly like this or just reacting to a new situation. You don't want to make excuses or give too many chances, so the "tuck it in your pocket" mechanism gives you some time to figure it out.

But . . . It's the Millennium

Since the advent of smartphone technology, people seem to be looking down at little screens all day long. While focused on your little screen, you'll not be aware of the life going on around you. Without this awareness, you can't *observe*. Therefore, before you can begin to hone your observation skills, you must *understand* the amount of time you spend with your technology and then *limit* it. For many, that seems impossible but if you do it in small increments, it not only becomes possible but you will feel as if a monkey has been taken off your back. When people learn to live with less technology, they start to feel a welcome sense of freedom.

If you're on a date, slow things down and really listen to the other person and note whether or not your date is listening to you. If you spend much of your day in rapid-fire texting mode, practice slowing it all down so you can return to active listening and thoughtful responses. One night I received a frantic call from client who said he had just spent ten hours talking to his ex. I thought, "Ten hours?! What did they talk about?" I expected a long, in-depth conversation covering many topics, but instead learned they been texting the entire time.

These two highly educated people said things in text that would not have been uttered on the phone or in person. He emailed me the text conversation. It was difficult to believe that these two, who held advanced degrees, had wasted an entire day exchanging inane, thoughtless communications. Did neither one of them think of picking up the phone to talk? You can only talk on the phone for so long. Even email becomes burdensome after a while. However, texting can go on for hours and accomplish nothing, as happened here.

Observation Is Necessary to Changing How You Interact with New Partners

Good relationships begin with paying attention. Attention starts with good observation skills. To increase your skills, I recommend journaling, which is writing down your thoughts and feelings for at least twenty minutes a day. Even if you have no idea what to write about, sit down and think about your day and your reactions and responses to different situations. Sometimes people say, "Journaling doesn't work for me." But usually it is they who have not worked at journaling. When you are journaling and observing your different responses to different situations, you become more aware of what you are doing when. If there are specific behaviors from others or events that trigger responses in you, you want to know it. You want to listen for and think about knee-jerk reactions, which you experience immediately without thinking. You may internally feel the pressure of a knee-jerk reaction, but you don't have to respond outwardly to it. You can pull back from immediate action. For example, fear of abandonment may rear its head when someone is late picking you up. Your tendency is to feel upset and yell or sulk when they get there. No excuse or reason is good enough for you. You may shout, "You know I have abandonment issues! What were you thinking by leaving me there and not answering my calls?" You may have gone through this several times with people. Now you observe this reaction in yourself and understand that it's ruined several relationships before. To combat this, affirm that you are okay no matter what and that you will be okay if your partner doesn't arrive and you just hope everything is all right. You take charge of your emotions instead of letting them take charge of you and expect someone else to soothe you. When you do this, you feel more in control of your life and less like a victim. By observing both yourself and others, you can be fully in command of your life and your reality.

When you go out, be aware of what your date is doing, saying, or not saying. Take note of shoulder shrugs, blank stares, and how polite your date is or isn't to other people. Does your date stare people down? Does your date check other people out? Does your date act rude to the valet? These are all things to note. If you're too busy tweeting that you just had a fabulous meal at a four-star restaurant, you may be missing the fact that you're with a one-star dud.

Honing Observation for Successful Dating and Personal Safety

In a healthy life, there is balance, self-control, and a sense of responsibility. Smartphones are incredibly handy, but don't use the "emergency" excuse to being forever wedded to your phone.

Emergencies don't come up that often, and being inattentive can put you in an emergency quicker than putting away the phone and being attentive can. It's fine to have your phone with you, but you don't need it twenty-four hours a day. As technology increases, observation becomes more of an effort than it ever has been. It's time to return to a time when phones were dumb and people were smart.

Before you start dating, spend time every day observing others. Being safe on dates is important, especially when you're meeting people from the Internet for the first time. If you're leaving a first date, it's important to keep a keen eye out and to look in your rear view mirror and side mirrors to note if the car behind you has been there a long time. Although the dangers of distractions from technology are very real, it's equally important for your emotional well-being that you start to take as much time as you can, every day, to enhance your observation skills.

Over the next four weeks, commit to a few things that will make you more observant and/or limit your use of technology. These suggestions come from clients who've found that paying more attention has increased their awareness and made their life happier:

1. I will not talk or text while driving (even hands-free talking); I will limit eating and drinking.
2. I will listen actively in a one-on-one conversation without distraction and without trying to think of what I'll say when the other person finishes.
3. I will pay attention to how many times I'm nodding or shaking my head or making a facial expression

that doesn't match what I'm thinking or feeling, to convey that I'm listening more than I am.

4. I will note the number of times I start speaking before someone has finished a sentence.

5. When I'm out walking, I'll look all around me and note what's new since the last time I walked there.

6. I will turn off my phone during dinner every night and ask others to do the same.

7. I will not entertain my children every second in the car or in public. I will explain to them that it's important to be aware and know what others are doing.

8. I will not start or end my day with distractions. I will sit quietly or listen to soft music for at least ten minutes before looking at my phone, computer, or television in the morning and turn everything off for a specific time at night.

9. While driving I will notice the cars behind me and around me. I will take note if someone seems to be following me and occasionally take a circuitous route to where I'm going.

10. I will affirm that staying attentive is important to being safe, healthy, and engaged.

At the end of four weeks, you should have decreased your use of technology and other distractions (such as television) to a surprising extent. Your listening skills should have improved, and you should feel more aware of everything that is happening around you. This skill will help you when you are meeting potential partners, their friends, and their families. Becoming a keen observer prior to getting into a relationship or in the early days of the relationship will give you clues you would otherwise miss.

Although many tell me that their partner just started to act incongruously toward the end of the relationship, most inventories reveal that there were clues from the start. In the blush of new love or the excitement of being with someone who seemed to care, however, it was overlooked. When you're committed to being observant, you can't overlook incongruous behavior, and you'll save yourself a lot of misery if you catch it early.

chapter 3

Preparation, Cultivation, and Boundary Setting

Samantha, 34 / It is so hard to walk away sometimes. Even though I "know better," it's tough when someone is holding you close after you've been alone for so long.

Jessica, 32 / After almost a year since my breakup, I started seeing a new guy who was tall, well spoken, and polite—all on my list. Then one day I was babysitting for my nieces and nephews and we were playing and he knocked my four-year-old niece over and she started crying. He told her she wasn't hurt and to stop crying— and he didn't even know her! That was it for me and that wasn't even something my horrible ex would have done. But I went home that night and added to the list:

Must treat my family with respect and care. You learn as
you go—what is and isn't okay for someone to do.

Cynthia, 44 / When I met my ex-boyfriend, he
seemed charming and wonderful. One night I said
that I didn't really like the restaurant he wanted to go
to on a Saturday night. It was loud and geared more
toward the mid-twenties crowd. He seemed to change
almost instantly, telling me that I was an angry woman
(I'm not), that nothing made me happy (until then I
hadn't complained about a thing), and that all women
were whiners and complainers. The last remark did me
in! He was projecting his past onto me and I realized
it was a HUGE red flag. I didn't want to spend my
life on the defensive. Been there, done that. He didn't
understand that I never wanted to see him again, but
I've learned it's not my place to make it make sense to
him. It's my place to take care of me.

The most important part of getting back out there is preparing for a different experience this time and remaining true to
your boundaries and standards. Question 4 helps you figure out
how to develop a new and different approach to dating and relationships and keep that change in the forefront of your mind
throughout the experience.

What does that mean? Simply put, it means taking a
new approach to dating and relationships where you have

prepared in several ways. You have changed your dating approach and mind-set, being sure that you are not in a place in your mind where you can easily fall back to old patterns. You will approach dating differently this time, armed with defenses against rejection or possible rebuke by someone you think you can care about. To be prepared for the world of dating, you must be realistic about its traps and pitfalls. You are no longer an innocent going out to the slaughterhouse but a sophisticated and careful thinker who will face dating and relationships on your terms and will not be bowed by any bumps in the road.

Question 5 is the most important. It has to do with developing and defining your boundaries and standards, which are imperative to creating loving and healthy relationships. It continues into the next chapter with "the list"—your guidelines for dating and starting new relationships.

Preparation and Cultivation

Question 4: Am I prepared to return to dating with a new mind-set to cultivate loving relationships?

When you're learning to observe others, you should be looking at them through the lens of what you want in your life now, not what you've had before. Getting back out there is scary, so being as prepared as possible is the key to successful post-breakup dating. To prepare for dating and getting into a healthy relationship, it's important to review your affirmations and choose the ones that will help you remain confident in any situation or develop some new ones. It's also important to review the beginnings of your former relationships and see what red flags you missed, what mistakes you made, what you forgave too early or too easily, and how you repeated those patterns. Preparation includes expanding your view of dating so that you don't dismiss a bad date out of hand if it may turn into a friendship or a business opportunity. Do not take such a narrow view of dating that it's simply the path to "the one." There is a lot to learn about yourself and others as you date.

Preparing for your return to dating includes developing a mind-set that you will enter relationships only with people who will expand your life scope and not keep you from the people and things that you love. Before you date, it's important to have hobbies, interests, and friends, and to make sure that they remain a central part of your life. A big red flag needs to go up whenever you find yourself relinquishing something or someone for a new person in your life. While you may not have room for everything you once did, you should be preparing a priority list of things you need to keep in your life to maintain your sanity and happiness. A young woman reports, "I had so many boyfriends in high school and college who were jealous of my friends, my guy friends, my career plans, any play, concert, or sporting event I went to without them, any field trip whether I had a good time or not, that I was determined to change it in grad school. If a guy showed jealousy about anything, I cut it off. I am much happier now that I have a nonjealous boyfriend, and I enjoy a great life with him and when I'm not with him."

Preparation Approach

Before you're ready to settle down with your forever love, chances are you'll have to make a temporary pit stop in the dating world. Many would prefer to not stop here but to just meet someone at the deli counter one day, strike up a conversation, and realize that your soul mate has arrived between the clerk calling numbers sixty-two and sixty-three. However, chances are slim that this will happen. If you're going to go "back out there" to date, it's time to rethink your old patterns and behaviors and prepare yourself mentally and emotionally.

The ritual of dating, mating, and relating is like nothing else. You'll find yourself on dates where you really like someone who doesn't like you, or someone really likes you when all you want to do is ask for the check. These experiences are more about the process than about you. To avoid a string of terrible first dates, another "started out well but was short-lived" relationship, or a long-term relationship with the wrong person, you must be well prepared this time around.

Affirm that you will pay attention to warnings even if everything is cozy and warm. Many new couples inhabit a cozy fantasy world the first few months. It's easy to be with someone who tells you how wonderful you are because nothing has put the relationship to a test. Some physical chemistry, a few similar interests, and the ability to make each other smile or laugh will result in a skewed version of the person and the relationship. The true test of a relationship comes when the chips are down, tensions run high, and you're both so stressed out that you want to move as far away from the relationship as possible.

A lack of interest in going further has more to do with where the other person is rather than a problem with you. There are many reasons why people don't pursue you or stay interested after the first date and a lot of it, in fact most of it, has nothing to do with you.

The most important attribute a person can have is being sincerely interested in you and your life. Being able to hold a conversation, tell a few jokes, or pick a good restaurant or movie does not a long-term relationship make. It's important that the person you are dating likes you and enjoys being with you. Leave the challenges behind. If you find yourself trying to woo or win someone over, it's time to pick someone else. This time around you want to be with a person who wants to be with you and no one else. Prepare to walk away, even if you're having fun, from someone who is not thrilled to have you as a choice. Being with someone who doesn't see your intrinsic value will erode your value.

Another way to prepare is to understand that dating may not lead to romance but can lead to friendships, networking opportunities, and other possibilities. A woman set up on a blind date by a friend wasn't interested in her date in a romantic way. However, as they started to talk, they learned that they knew some of the same people and were interested in expanding their businesses. Although their businesses were very different, they exchanged phone numbers and contacts, and each helped the other meet people who could help them in their line of work.

She laughs when she talks about it: "I think my friend was right on the money when she thought we had things in common, but there was no physical attraction or chemistry. We've not only remained close friends, but we've helped each other's businesses grow in so many ways." In dating preparation, remember that you're not only looking for love but also connections, contacts, and people to count on. If a friend fixes you up, there's a chance you'll find something worth keeping.

Preparation also involves understanding that this time has to be different. You may have fallen in love with your ex shortly after you met. Perhaps this time around it's not going to be that easy. Don't spend the end of every first date dwelling on how easy it was to fall in love with your ex, but how hard it is now. Remember, finding the wrong one takes a lot less effort than finding the right one.

Your dating preparation includes developing a keen awareness of the potential pitfalls and drama that can occur as well as protecting yourself when you're feeling emotional, unattractive, or unwanted. Prepare for the times when you're going to feel hopeless, when you feel that no one is ever going to love you again. Prepare for times of loneliness or for when someone suddenly breaks off a budding relationship for no reason that you can fathom. Preparing yourself for all possible scenarios is essential before you start to date. One of the most useful exercises I go through with my newly dating clients involves making "even though" statements. It's another form of affirmation to take the worst situation and turn it into a positive learning experience. Some examples of "even though" statements include:

- Even though this date didn't work out, I'm still attractive.
- Even though this attractive person didn't respond in kind to my advances, I am still lovable.
- Even though [name] is not calling me back, I'm still a fantastic person who is giving, loving, and kind.
- Even though [name] didn't give us a chance, someone is out there who will see the wonderful and cheerful person I am and want to be with me.
- Even though I was interested in pursuing things with someone not interested in me, I'm still strong in my conviction that I'm desirable.
- Even though I don't have a date this weekend, I'm still worthwhile.
- Even though I feel lonely tonight, I know I'm a good catch and someone great will see that too.

Start to prepare your "even though" affirmations and you'll find them extremely helpful when you're dating. This prepares you for all situations so that you are okay no matter what.

Cultivation

Cultivation is continuing your observations of the world around you, including your date and yourself. It's important to continue the work even when you're on top of the world or looking forward to another date with a terrific person. Cultivation is an important part of the plan in which you continue to journal, affirm, observe, and prepare.

If your initial excursions into the world of dating don't go well, it's not time to freak out or think that it's a sign that no one is going to want you ever again. Keep cultivating a positive mind-set that you're learning and growing with each date, even if it's a bad date. Try to take something from each date and keep cultivating a mind-set that you're not going to settle, you're going to keep yourself safe, and that it's more important to know who you are and what you're doing than to find Mr. or Ms. Right the minute you step back out into the world.

If you feel upset or rejected, or if you're missing your ex or thinking you're going to be alone forever, it's time to bring back your positive self-talk and affirmations. If you feel yourself sliding back, start to affirm: "I'm a good person who is worthy of love and caring," and "When I am the right person, the right person for me will come along." You have to cultivate your self-image, your confidence, and your positive outlook. You have to use the affirmations that you've developed in order to deal with dating.

Positive self-talk is the center of cultivation. If you begin to feel anxious that your partner is about to leave and you're going to be left in a mess on the floor, then you need to go back to all the tools that have given you the self-confidence to know that you'll be okay no matter what. If you come out of a dating situation that has beaten your self-esteem or you've been sideswiped by a lunatic pretending to be normal, then you have to go back to the observation, preparation, and cultivation that got you this far in the first place. Going back to the basics will always put you back on track. No matter what the situation, know that you have the tools and the ability to learn from the situation and move on to a better one.

Boundaries and Standards

Question 5: Will I remain true to my boundaries and standards even when feeling swept up in falling in love again?

Love and trust are the key ingredients in all deep and lasting commitments. But before you can create a lasting bond with another, you must make a commitment to yourself. Knowing yourself includes knowing your boundaries well enough to enter into a relationship with your eyes wide open, and loving and trusting yourself gives you the tools to enforce those boundaries. It's imperative that you honor the commitment to yourself to accept only loving and respectful people in your life. If I had to name one area where my clients actually feel themselves getting healthier in their mate selection, it is when they begin to define their reasonable expectations and draw boundaries with everyone in their lives.

Those who have been hurt in past relationships talk about trust issues that can be an enormous barrier to intimacy. Several of my clients insist they can't get close to people because they fear being hurt again. However, there is no way to find emotional connectedness with another person unless you bring down your walls to some degree and attach on some emotional level. If you're not ready to put yourself out there and take a chance on being hurt, you're not ready to date again. One way to trust yourself is to know your boundaries and standards, and be prepared to leave if something that's very important to you—one of your boundaries—is compromised.

Trust is something that is earned. Too many expect to feel warm, loved, and secure and when they are, they take this as evidence that they're with a person they can trust. When you first start dating, it's natural to want to jump into future scenarios to see if this is the person for you. However, it's impossible to tell from the start if this person is trustworthy. You may be able to guess, based on what they've said about their past, but you need to accept that it's also based on your own perception and ability to heed warning signs.

If you don't know who you are, what you want, and where you are going, you aren't going to succeed in a relationship. To figure out if you and your partner look at life the same way, you must first figure out how you yourself look at it. You must know your boundaries and standards. You must know when to say no and mean it, and how not to be worn down by someone badgering you to say yes. You must know how to say, "The answer is no and that's that."

Review Warning Signs That You Ignored in Past Relationships

Review your life inventory again, and you may recall times where you were at a crossroads and didn't know where to go or how to react. There may have been events, seemingly insignificant at the time, which indicated bigger problems to come. A friend said that when she was falling in love with her ex-husband, he told her that he didn't believe in evolution. Years later that conversation would come back to haunt her, as it represented the many beliefs he held that differed from hers. "I know it sounds crazy," she said, "but if I had explored that one thing we disagreed on, I would have found that we looked at life completely differently." She was too caught up in the chemistry of a whirlwind romance to put it through a reality test.

Though fraught with signs that there were going to be major issues, they continued at their feverish pace and went "all in" prematurely. Red flags were waving, sirens were wailing, and neon lights were flashing a warning. When you're looking for a life partner, it's not about finding someone you like, as there are many of those to be found; or even someone with whom you have toe-curling chemistry with, as there are many of those too; but about finding someone who will make a good team player and is good to you and for you. Many dates would make a good friend or good person to know or a temporary mate—but not a good life partner. Knowing what you want and having those qualities prioritized is an important step to understanding what kind of person will be compatible with you.

Examples of Warning Signs

When I talk about warning signs or "red flags," often a client has to think hard about those present in the beginning of the last relationship. Most only remember how much in love they were, how great the sex was, or how wonderful it was to feel included in someone's family or with someone's friends. Often a new relationship opens up a completely new world and you are swept away by the feelings of being in love and exploring this new world. However, often there are signs, sometimes subtle and sometimes very pronounced, that clue you in that there will be trouble later.

A client's mother had passed and he was, appropriately, an emotional mess. Yet his fiancée, who he had been with almost a year, saw emotional displays as a sign of weakness. She gave him some space for a week or so, but then began to complain that he wasn't there for her. When he talked about his grief, she told him to pull himself together and get on with life. To summarize her response would be to say that she abandoned him when he needed her the most. When we first started talking about it, he could not see that at all. The problem here, as with many people, is he did not know what was appropriate. Should he tend to his grief or to his fiancée? I had to convince him that expressing grief after the death of a loved one is appropriate and it is reasonable to be unavailable to the relationship for a time. Her lack of understanding was unreasonable—and showed a flaw in her ability to express empathy or care.

In looking for a partner, you're looking for someone who can see you as part of a team that faces life together. When life gets tough for one or both of you, you don't get angry at each other or pull away. You face it together without blame, accusations, or taking your emotions out on the person closest to you. This requires empathy and kindness. Sometimes it's hard to figure out if this is there in the beginning, but if you're observant and able to see how supportive and caring someone is during early times, you can get a glimpse of how they are going to be later on. For my client whose girlfriend wanted him to get over his mother's death right away, any of his emotional expressions were unacceptable to her long before his mother passed. This is because she was self-centered and not other-oriented at all. If you watch for red flags, you can usually pick up on this before a major life event occurs.

Another client expressed to the woman he was seeing that he was uncomfortable when she talked about other men she was dating. He wanted an exclusive relationship with her, understood she was not ready for one, but said he would appreciate if she stopped talking about other men. She apologized but then said that his boundary was adding more stress to her life. If you set a reasonable boundary and someone pushes back on it, even if the person begrudgingly agrees to it, you need to take note. His request was reasonable, and he tried to be as understanding as possible. He said, "I get it, I just don't want to hear about it all the time." Her response indicated that his request stressed her because now she had to be careful about what she said to him. Someone who is not adult enough to realize a filter is needed in certain situations is not going to be a good and loving partner. Some people are naturally self-centered and some are clinically narcissistic, and you must listen carefully for these things early in a relationship. The lack of response to a reasonable request is one of those things. If you state what you need and there is pushback or noncompliance with a reasonable request, pay attention to that.

Boundaries Are Necessary
but Difficult to Enforce

Boundaries can be tough to learn and enforce, but they teach the world how to treat you. They show where your lines are, and if you are sincere about your boundaries not being crossed, they won't be. When people know your boundaries, they know how to behave around you. When others have no clear sense of what you will and won't put up with, they test the limits. This is true of relatively nice people and new people who have not yet received the message as to what is and is not okay with you.

Healthy people respect people with boundaries because it guides them into the best interaction possible. A healthy person does not want to do anything that threatens a budding relationship or friendship. A healthy person wants to know another's wants and needs to see if they are compatible and if not, why not? Is this something that can be fixed or not? These are questions a healthy person is open to and interested in having answered truthfully. Healthy people do not want "square peg/round hole" relationships. They are interested only in being with those who are a good fit. Knowing everyone's boundaries answers that question quickly.

When you are out with a new person, it may feel strange to set a boundary or say no to someone you know only superficially. You're out to have a good time, light conversation, and fun, so to express an opinion your date doesn't share may ruin a nice evening. If your date is a healthy person, your input will be welcomed when asked if you like sushi and you don't.

If you say, "I don't really like sushi; I'd prefer something else," a healthy person will respect your preference. If your date is persistent or asks, "Have you ever actually tried sushi?" that's usually a clue that you can expect a hard time about other things as well.

The way a person responds to minor boundary setting is important because it gives you a clue about likely responses to major boundaries. Take note if someone who hardly knows you is trying to talk you into something you don't want. Many who struggle to set boundaries have always been "soft" or "push-overs," though they would describe themselves as "generous" or "wanting to pay it forward" or some other rationalization or justification. Generosity does not come from needing to be thought of as nice or wanting to be liked. That is not true generosity but manipulation designed to make people think highly of you. Truly generous people give out of a spirit of giving, and they have strong boundaries to avoid being taken advantage of. If you do not set boundaries, people will mistake your kindness for weakness. You will play the fool and give too much to too many for too long, leaving you exhausted and broke and unable to give to those who really need it.

A client insisted she felt bad for her ex so she kept buying him things and told me how "generous" she was. I said, "If you want to be generous and give to people who deserve it, donate to cancer research, a domestic violence organization, a homeless shelter, or an animal rescue—places that need and deserve donations. Your partner is not a charity and if you treat someone like one, you will be burned in the end. So rethink your "generosity" and shore up your boundaries to keep yourself safe from those who only want to take advantage of you.

It's Okay to Have Boundaries

Strong boundaries result in good relationships, high self-esteem, and emotional well-being. Without them, it is impossible to work toward a loving relationship with a healthy partner because you get lost and fail to understand where you begin and others leave off. In literature on codependency, boundaries are often the most challenging thing to understand and implement, yet they make the difference between healthy relationships and codependent relationships. Not only are boundaries okay, but a healthy relationship cannot exist without them.

Before dating, take time to figure out what is and is not okay with you and what you need in a relationship. The goal is to set a boundary and stick to it. Affirm your right to say no and your right to have reasonable expectations of others. As Melody Beattie says, "We cannot simultaneously set a boundary and take care of another person's feelings." Therefore, it is imperative you develop affirmations that enforce your right to have boundaries. Some examples from clients and readers include:

I have the right to set boundaries.
I have the right to say no.
I have the right to have my voice heard.
I have the right to ask others to be on time.
I have the right to stop bailing everyone out.

I have the right to allow others to experience the logical or
   natural consequences of their actions.
I have the right to set a boundary regardless of how others feel
   about it.
I have the right to expect fair and respectful treatment from
   others.

You cannot get into another relationship or friendship or be around your family or co-workers without knowing that you can keep yourself safe. Fearfulness is a sign of not having boundaries. If you have good boundaries, you know how to convey that to the world and keep yourself safe. Saying no or refusing to capitulate does not make you petty, small, or vengeful. If you need to say no for self-protection, that is all you need to worry about. When faced with a situation that calls for it, affirm that "I need to say no to protect myself. Saying no is okay to protect myself." It's hard at first, but do it! Healthy people will respect you, and unhealthy people will drop away. It will change your life for the better.

The reason to spend so much time on setting boundaries, changing standards, and enforcing limits is that this is where my clients feel "the work" kicking in. Almost every client I have begins to understand that they are changing and getting healthy when they realize they are setting boundaries and staying true to their standards. Even if it takes a while, when the day comes that they're aware that they have stopped shifting lines in the sand, they are almost gleeful that they have taken charge of their own life. Without these solid lines, relationships continue to be painful and confusing.

The Three-Time Rule

Someone once asked me how many chances are proper to give when setting boundaries. Unless it's infidelity or abuse—where you allow zero second chances—I suggest implementing the "three-time rule." The general guideline is that you ask for something twice and if the other doesn't comply, then you must make a decision on the third occasion. After three times, you are negotiating with yourself, as Melody Beattie says. Negotiating with yourself is another term for lowering your standards—the one thing you must never do. On the third strike, the person is out.

Chapter 4 continues this discussion with the standards and compatibility list that will guide you to recognize what you need and want from yourself and another person in your next relationship. Some of the discussion will loop back to boundaries, as it's impossible to discuss nonnegotiable items without bringing boundaries into it again. Many think they are failing at relationships when they are actually failing at boundaries and standards. Chapter 4 looks at developing your standards and compatibility list so that both your boundaries and standards are clear before you step back out into the world of dating and relationships.

chapter 4

The Standards and Compatibility List

Peter, 41 / At first my list was, as I was, all screwed up. I wanted someone to take care of me and not have any of her own accomplishments or interests. When I saw that broken out on the "Other" side of the list, I could see my side needed work. I was glad to be able to see, in black and white, why my previous relationships failed and what I needed to do to make it right.

Victoria, 35 / The thought of having a list and holding myself accountable to leave if someone didn't meet up with the standards on the list was so hard for me to grasp. It took me many months of continually dating

the wrong people before I decided to sit down and
give it a try. But I was surprised when it made a huge
difference.

Eleanor Roosevelt said, "Know what you stand for or you'll fall
for anything." The readers and clients quoted above are referring
to a list I suggest to those about to embark upon dating. The
compatibility and standards list constitutes the code of behavior you expect from yourself and others. To adhere to the code
and expect others to do the same, you must carefully develop—
based on experience and future expectations—how you want to
be treated and commit to releasing anyone who does not adhere
to or respect your code. Once you are clear on that, you know
where you are going and who is going with you. Before you go
out there, it's time to decide what you want and what you need.

You will develop your list by deciding what is negotiable
and nonnegotiable, acceptable and unacceptable. You will also
tackle a gray area known as "may be negotiable." This category
is reserved for some items that may be negotiable if someone is
amazing in other areas. One woman said, "I lived with a slob
for many years. When I went back to dating, I wanted someone
who didn't leave shaving clippings in the sink and didn't throw
his clothes on the floor. I thought this was nonnegotiable. But
when I met my husband, he was so wonderful and generous
with me, my kids, and my pets, I didn't care if he left shaving
clippings all over the house. That moved into my 'negotiable'
column but only for him. If I had to start over again, it would
go back to my 'nonnegotiable' column." It is important, when

moving items from one column to the next one, you are doing it because someone is, as this woman says, "so wonderful" and not because you think you can change him. This chapter will also explore the "accept it, change it, or leave" concept that will help you with the gray areas of what you will and will not accept. This chapter is devoted to preparing a new mind-set toward dating and then preparing your list of what you want in a relationship. It's better to be armed and knowledgeable than to be confused and careless about what it is you want and who can or cannot provide it.

How to Create Your List

Like your daily affirmations, your list serves to remind you what you need to be and what to look for in others. Some of my clients create their list on the computer or in a notebook. Some keep it in a journal and some on a piece of paper near their bed or bathroom mirror. Some speak it into their phone and listen to it later. Some of my clients make a list on a piece of paper with a line drawn down the middle that has *Me* written on one side and *You* on the other side to stay aware of what they want in themselves and in a partner. Others do a "vision board" or collage project where they cut out words and images to represent what they are bringing into it. One client wanted a cultured woman as her next partner and made a board with museums and art galleries on it as well as a functional to-do list for herself of Meetup.com groups and community groups that she wanted to join to improve her chances of meeting a future partner. She added things she didn't want such as smoking and beer drinking and tacked up a photo of a cigarette and of beer and drew large Xs through them. For a while, the collage became bigger and more refined as she thought about it more. Another client who played tennis wanted that to be very important to his next mate so right in the middle, he pasted a large tennis racquet. Another wanted a man who would open doors for her and she found a photo of that. Whatever written methods or visuals speak to you is what you should use.

A client who joined an online dating service went to an educational supply store and bought gold and silver stars as well as red and pink flags and a corkboard with the names of men she was seeing. The stars and flags were of differing sizes. If she felt someone was less than honest with her, on her chart she put a big red flag. If she wasn't sure and it needed more investigation, she would make it a pink one with a question mark. One time a man she was seeing became drunk and belligerent to the waitress, and she went home prepared to give him a big red flag when she decided that she'd had enough and just removed his name. She said, "Until I started a visual representation of what someone was doing, it wasn't very clear. Staring at it every morning gave me a good idea of where things were heading."

Everyone has a different way of doing it; don't be afraid to experiment. Visual aids can help people understand what is going on. How you represent what you're seeing in yourself and those you're dating is up to you. Whatever way you choose, it's important that your standards and boundaries are represented concretely. Once you are dating, you will need to refer to it regularly, so be sure it's handy.

The "Me" Side of the List

The first part of the list should be clear and written from the perspective of "past mistakes" you have made and don't want to repeat, such as the woman who dated smokers and then realized she had too much against the addiction to be with a smoker. So her "me" side included a cigarette struck through by a large, red X, which represented her intolerance for a future partner's behavior. So the "me" side should include your own behavior as well as a future partner's behavior.

A client said she was guilty of the freeze out and silent treatment. When she looked back at the impatience some of her boyfriends had shown, she realized that she needed to take a time-out when she became angry at them instead of screaming at them to leave her alone. We worked on her behavior as well as her need for space when she felt stressed out. I encouraged her to explain to future partners that when she felt overly emotional, she needed some time and space to calm down, using "I" language, which will be explained in Chapters 9–10. For now, an example of "I" language is, "I am feeling very upset right now, and I am having trouble pulling my thoughts together. I would like a little while to compose myself." This is preferable to, "You are making me crazy! Get away from me before I explode!" Instead of ostracizing someone who cares and wants to make things better, she learned to simply take a break, come back, and calmly talk it out.

Her side of the list included explaining her need to cool off when angry and a reminder on the "you" side of the list to check on her boyfriend's impatience. As she worked to change her behavior, she had no idea if a man's impatience in the past was caused by her behavior or if she had a habit of picking impatient men. She put a big question mark around the word "impatience."

A *GPYB* reader wrote, "In many of my adult relationships, the man was newly separated. I thought, originally, that this indicated that I was a caretaker and wanted to help soothe someone's wounds, but it wasn't that at all. I found I had commitment issues and so long as I was with a newly separated person, I didn't worry about being much more than a girlfriend." Some who have been the "other woman" or the "other man" have discovered similar fears of intimacy. "There was no reason I spent those years waiting for him to leave his wife," said one seminar attendee, "except that I knew he wouldn't." It was clear that she stayed involved with a married man for so long because she had her own intimacy issues and didn't really want a full-time lover. For the longest time she portrayed herself as a victim of sorts, dazzled beyond all reason, by a man who talked a good game and promised her the moon, the sun, and the stars as soon as he extricated himself from his wife. However, the bottom line was that no matter what his excuses, he wasn't leaving his wife; the other woman was not a victim but a volunteer who refused to look at her own intimacy issues.

Each of them worked on the "me" list and found that "unavailable because they are still attached to someone else" was prevalent throughout the lists. A woman who made a visual representation of it was stunned to see so many negatives and red flags in all the men she had been involved with. She kept the board up as a reminder for what she needed to work on. So when you look at your own patterns in relationships, be sure to note what things you not only accepted but looked for in the past.

Next, your list should also include warning signs and red flags you missed in prior relationships. My friend who missed the evolution discussion said, "Had I pushed him on that, as I did later, I would have learned so many things about him that would have been good to know. He not only believed many things that I thought ridiculous, but he would get angry in ways that hinted at a malevolent personality. Had I pushed some of these nonpersonal, scientific discussions a bit further, I would have seen the underlying anger and intolerance that eventually bubbled to the surface." It's easy to write, "Must be tolerant and not have anger issues" on the "you" side of the board, but you also have to take responsibility for glossing over the indications of unacceptable behavior and note that on your side of the board. For every action, there is a reaction or a nonreaction and that must be noted. Own your old behavior; otherwise, you may be doomed to repeat it.

If you are paying attention to the "you" side of the board and start to notice issues that could be a problem later on and choose to ignore them, you set yourself up for misery. A budding romance can feel wonderful, but it's important to remain true to what you do and do not want in a future partner. It is important to note every missed sign from past relationships so that you don't repeat them. Pushing an issue in the early going may feel uncomfortable, but when you compare it to years of "if only I had . . ." the discomfort should become bearable. Making lists and taking notes may be the last thing you want to do when a new romance is in the air. But had you done it in the past, it might have saved you a lot of aggravation.

As you look back on your past, there may be things you regret about your own behavior. If you were withholding, critical, blaming, passive-aggressive, and so on, it's time to examine that behavior and make an effort to change it. You want to find the right person, but first you must be the right person. If you have anger issues or fears that surface in a dysfunctional way, it's time to look at that and work to learn the proper way of dealing with anger, fear, and past hurts. You may need to develop affirmations and mantras to soothe yourself when you become upset or project that someone is going to hurt you. You may also have gone to the other extreme, biting your tongue when you should have spoken out or being too generous with your time, money, or understanding. If you've been a doormat, you have to own that as well.

Another area to examine is what you have and have not accepted and how reasonable or unreasonable you have been. Sometimes it's just a matter of changing the people you've been with and sometimes changing yourself, but it's usually a bit of both. Review your past and use this information to include things about you and your life that should be accepted by someone else, and what things you want to find in a partner.

A blog reader had children but her boyfriend barely engaged with them. Everything else seemed great so she decided to talk to him about it. He said, matter-of-factly, "I don't really like kids." Although he was a terrific boyfriend, her kids were too important for her to continue the relationship. However, she could have found this out much earlier if she had emphasized her children's importance. A nonparent who doesn't like kids may tolerate them for your sake, but if you want someone who will talk with them and interact on a deeper level, you need to emphasize this before you get too far. Though this issue may belong on both sides of the list, it's up to you to decide what questions need answers before you get further along. Whether parent or nonparent, you should think about where kids fit into your life before you date. When I was dating after my divorce, my children felt as if they were competing, and losing the competition, with step-siblings (my ex's new wife's kids). In light of that, I refused to seriously date a man with children until they were older and then I met Michael. Many men with children assumed I would be open to dating them when I was not. It was hard to explain, but it was on my list of nonnegotiables. My kids already felt they were losing one parent to another person's children, and I refused to ask them to accommodate more potential step-siblings. This item went on both the "me" side of the list, and the "you" side of the list (further discussed in the next section.) For me it was about being upfront about not dating men with children, and for them it was about not having children. It also cancels out dealing with ex-wives and girlfriends, as there should be no reason for a man without children to be in touch with his ex. If he was, that was another thing that was unacceptable and nonnegotiable.

These are hard questions that are tough to look at and talk about early on, but doing so avoids unnecessary clashes. When you're first dating, "real life" is not intruding so you have to create scenarios for your date to see if you both envision being together outside the somewhat fabricated backdrop of those first dinner dates or walks in the park. Your list can serve as a lens through which you look at the people you are dating.

The "You" Side of the List

Now you have completed your side of the list and can see what you neglected to look at and you have given weight to your own behavior in the past, it's time to make a list with regard to others. Start a list with the headings: *absolutely unacceptable, must have, negotiable,* and *maybe negotiable.* Again, you can write this out or make it a visual, collage-type representation, but it needs to be in writing, not just in your head. The list may contain very broad images and phrases, but be sure to "drill down" and make the images and words have as much meaning as possible.

As time goes on, you will find yourself making additions and subtractions to this list. Dating again must be approached, at first, as a learning experience or else you will put too much stock into everyone who comes along. The person you must take the most stock in, at this fragile juncture, is *you.* There is no sense in wasting precious time or hoping to change someone. Know what you want, know what you need, and then spend time with people who can give you what you want and need. Sometimes a person's true qualities do not become apparent until later on, so learn to take a wait-and-see approach. Don't dive into relationships without knowing if a person has a clue as to how to treat another or has qualities that come close to meeting the items on your list.

From the start, you should be observing others and taking in as much information as you can. Whether you like it or not, you must step back and allow someone to show you the person under the exterior. Take note when someone is surly with wait staff, valets, or store clerks. Someone trying to impress you but failing to be courteous to strangers is unimpressive. Observe if the person is oversharing about life or sharing important matters that are appropriate only in a long-term relationship situation. Another observation to make is sketchiness about subjects that are normally shared, such as job, education, family, or interests. Someone may be shy or not interested in sharing until you are better acquainted, which is a good idea, but take note of it. There are many areas, like levels of communication, which may be hard to gauge in the beginning, but more concrete areas can be ascertained clearly.

Items on the list that are clear should be adhered to no matter what. One client's list started with "honesty." It was starred, highlighted, and bracketed with exclamation points. But a few dates left her feeling starry-eyed, and when her new love revealed past dishonesty, she ignored it. It is a common ploy to secure the care of someone and then reveal things that otherwise would have caused the relationship to end the first night. If something troubling comes up, ask yourself, "Would I have gone out on a second date if this had been revealed on the first date?" You should observe as much as you can and figure out if what you see comports with your list and if it doesn't, commit that you will leave the situation and not try to change it. Leaving may hurt, but you have the tools, the knowledge, and the wherewithal to heal and move on. What you *don't* do is change your list to fit the current love interest. If honesty is truly the most important thing to you, a dishonest person needs to be shown the door as soon as the dishonesty becomes apparent.

Negotiable and Nonnegotiable

It's important to know what is *negotiable* and *nonnegotiable* and get this distinction straight in your head before you meet someone. You can develop your list from past relationships and things that really bothered you or you can date someone new and find something new to put on the list. You list should include *absolutely unacceptable* behaviors, such as verbal, mental, or physical abuse; mental illness; and addiction. Even if you have not encountered this before or if you have and think you're past it, write it down. As time goes on, you will most likely add to this list. Another list to make is *must have,* which can include basics such as a job and a car, but can also include a divorce decree, own apartment, love for animals, and the like. Think about all the things that could possibly be on these two lists and be sure they are there.

Next, go through your lists and tag each item as *negotiable, nonnegotiable,* and *maybe negotiable.* Of course abuse is nonnegotiable, but many times people are not sure what abuse looks like. They will not accept a punch in the face, but will accept being called names or belittled. It's important to list out "belittled" or "being called names" so that abuse as a nonnegotiable has meaning and substance. Otherwise, a broad phrase may obscure what it really means.

We did this exercise in a seminar, and one attendee had "mind-reading" on his list of nonnegotiables. I asked him what it meant as I wanted everyone to flesh their list out as much as possible, getting down to the fine details. He said, "I was always arguing with my ex-wife over what I was thinking. That's crazy. The minute a woman tells me what I'm thinking or that my behavior is saying something it's not, I'm out of there. I won't live on the defensive." I had him spell that out, "Will not tell me what I'm thinking or what my behavior means." A woman in the same seminar was dating a man who said things were going too quickly and that he had to pull back and maybe see other people. She argued in favor of exclusivity for a while but finally threw up her hands and said, "Okay, I'll see other people too." Then he accused her of playing games. She included a picture of a pretzel on her board with an X through it to represent twisted logic. Under that I had her quote a few of his phrases. Other recipients of pretzel logic wrote out the kinds of things that have been said to them so they learn to listen for it on dates and early in relationships.

Make a decision to walk away when you hear things that indicate a deep disconnect between the person you are dating and the partner you need. One man described his early relationship in this way: "My life was my problem, and her life was my problem. Nothing was her problem and when I screwed something up, terror rained down on me. I kept thinking I could make it better, but for two years, it only got worse." The question is, Why did he stay for two years? The answer is, he was caught up in the "trying to please" syndrome and lost sight of what he wanted. In every phase of a relationship, it is important to step back and review the quality of the partnership. On his list he wrote, "Yours? Mine? Or Ours? Who owns this problem?" to remind himself not to try to solve his partner's problems for her. He said that just asking that question has served him well in his subsequent endeavors. Based on your past, what are the questions you need to ask before partnering with someone? Make sure those questions show up on the list.

When you are dating and sexually active, consider the chance of unplanned pregnancy, or you may find yourself tethered to a questionable person for at least eighteen years. One woman said, "I helped him hide income from his ex-wife and then when we broke up, I had to chase him for child support. I didn't even know that 'first children come first' as far as most courts are concerned. Therefore, if anyone managed to find his money, his first wife would get it for their three children before I would. He was a terrible person who convinced me that his ex-wife was greedy and had enough of her own money and didn't need his, which was far from the truth." Most people do not get such a clear heads-up before a pregnancy, but those who do tend to ignore those signs. It's a huge price to pay for something that is fairly obvious. There is no reason to be the next in a series of people who get taken for a ride.

Now that you have your list, you have a set of instructions and codes ready for a new relationship or potential partner. When you allow someone to subject you to unacceptable treatment, you are hurting yourself. When you accept unacceptable behavior, it doesn't get any better. If you have a partner who is repeating the same mistreatment no matter how many promises were made or excuses were given, it becomes your responsibility to realize it is not changing and it's time to walk.

Accept It, Change It, or Leave

In every situation there are only three possible actions.

1. Accept it.
2. Change it.
3. Leave.

That's it. You can decide not to decide, but eventually you have to accept one of the options. Accepting a situation and leaving will be discussed further in Chapter 8.

Changing It

When you encounter something that is difficult to accept about another person, you can talk it out. If change is not a possibility, you are back to acceptance or leaving. You need to decide which one it is. If you have made your list and a commitment to yourself, you can figure out when you need to leave. Without the list, there are lies we all tell ourselves to rationalize unacceptable behavior. However, even if it were true, it doesn't mean it has to be true for you. A friend who is clearly uncomfortable with pornography said, "All men watch it. I just make sure it's not around the kids." First, it's not true that all men watch it and if you want no porn to be a standard of yours, then make it a standard and put it on the list. Many are upfront about it and others not so much, but you can ask and not be afraid of looking unreasonable if you state that something is not okay for you. If it's a deal breaker, then it's good to know it sooner rather than later.

Another man told his girlfriend, "I like to flirt and mean nothing by it. If it makes you uncomfortable, it's because you're insecure, not that I'm doing anything wrong." However, she considered it wrong and felt ashamed when they were out and he flirted with a waitress, a hostess, or other women at an event. Many times women would look at her with sympathy. Whenever she brought it up, he told her it was her problem and she needed to get over it. His rationalization was that if he went home with her at the end of the night, that's all she had to worry about. He told her the flirting meant nothing. One night he said, "If I don't go home with you, there's a problem. If I do, then there's no problem, I'm just being friendly." He wouldn't change and she couldn't accept it, so she ultimately realized she had to leave.

No, Just No

If your list includes "no porn" or "no flirting," then that's your standard. Many would find this to be reasonable, so don't change your standards so someone can fit into your life. If you're not okay with something, you should not be talked into it or made to explain it. This is a "no, just no" item. "No" is a one-word sentence and is not up for discussion. While there are "yes, just yes" items, most people aren't asked to explain them.

Even if there is chemistry but your *must haves* or your *non-negotiable unacceptables* are not honored, you know you can end it early and move along. This person is a virtual stranger, and there is no need to explain yourself. If it won't work unless you break yourself in two, then you want to end it. If someone hounds you and says you're being unreasonable, that is more evidence of a nonworkable relationship.

How Have You Conducted Your Life Until Now?

You need to have an idea of what you want in a person and how he or she lived before you met. A fundamental requirement for a relationship is that you respect your partner and the choices your partner has made in life. Someone may lose a job or file for bankruptcy because the stock market went south, but it's a whole other thing is someone is behind on child support because of anger at the ex-spouse or has criminal charges pending for vandalizing the property of an ex.

A good partner is a responsible person who has life necessities covered. A good partner is one who has a decent apartment, a decent job, and no outstanding issues with the law. If you live in an area where a car is needed, a license in good standing and a registered car should be a given. Your standard should be that any person, man or woman, supports the children they bring into the world. You make the children; you have an obligation to support those children. If your new love can't get that right, there is a moral compass issue. If you don't have "pays child support on time" on your standards list, you're going to be scraping the very bottom of the barrel.

Make sure you believe someone from the start. Doubts about veracity early in a relationship spell trouble. It's easy to give the benefit of the doubt once or twice, but if you are never sure what to believe, spare yourself the pain and get out. It's hard to leave when you're not sure, but if someone exaggerates or lies by omission, you deserve so much better than that. You didn't go through the pain of leaving your last relationship and working on yourself just to be with a chronic "untruth" teller. If you're getting signals early in the relationship, time to get out and stay out. There is no way to accept lies and usually no way to change a liar, so you have to choose "leave."

Lesser Issues

Many of my clients complain about things that are sure to cause major disagreement later on, especially unreliability or an inability to make solid plans. Others complain about minor arrangement issues with the person's ex or children. Still others don't want to be the one to make plans or take responsibility for aspects of a relationship that should be give and take. Even in these areas of "lesser" importance, boundaries and standards come into play. Some people are naturally good at planning and others are not; some can tolerate lateness in a person and others cannot. Before you go back out there, you want to address as many minor issues as you can. There will be new ones, and you're going to need to figure out how you feel about them. Is it negotiable or nonnegotiable? Is it acceptable or unacceptable? Is it a deal breaker or maybe just a bend in the road? As new things with new people come up, you need to understand where you stand on it and what it means for your future. Add it to your list under negotiable or nonnegotiable.

Reasonable and Unreasonable

It's challenging to step back once you're in the throes of romance, so you must be very clear about what you want in a future partner and relationship before you go back out there. Making lists, collages, or vision boards may seem to take all the passion and intrigue out of your romantic dalliances. However, as the examples above demonstrate, people can become muddled when they are unclear or unsure. So adhere to your list and continue to write down what is acceptable or unacceptable, negotiable or nonnegotiable in a future relationship. For example:

> *Person should be legally divorced.*
> *Person should make child support payments on time.*
> *Person should have a job.*
> *I will not allow anyone to call me names.*
> *I will not allow anyone to insult me.*
> *I will not allow anyone to disrespect my children.*
> *I will not date anyone who does not like animals.*

It is also important to note preferences that aren't necessarily deal breakers.

> *Someone interested in the theater.*
> *Someone who has never been married.*
> *Someone who has a close family.*

Another thing is red flags; promise yourself that you will leave if you see certain red flags.

>*I will leave if someone stands me up.*
>*I will leave if someone calls me a name.*
>*I will leave if someone shows signs of a bad temper.*

When you return to the world of dating with your lists, you are trying to answer the question, "Is this good enough?" If the answer is no, you set out to see if you need to accept it, change it, or leave. It's so much easier to work through the selection process this way instead of flailing about.

Moving Forward

When you're in between relationships, when you're even in between dates, and it doesn't seem like there's anyone out there or anyone who's a possibility, and times are tough and frustrating, look back on your life and look at the opportunities you've had during times when other doors closed. Remember the times where things worked out for you when you were sure they weren't going to. It's important to stay positive about the future and about the doors that are not yet ready to open. You must believe in yourself and believe that life is going to get better. "When one door closes, another opens" is not a trite cliché; it really is true that new opportunities become available when we lose certain things and people in our lives. Having your list combined with good boundaries helps you maintain your opportunities for good things to come into your life.

To start a healthy relationship, you need to know what you want in a partner. You must love yourself before you can love someone else. Loving yourself means that you know that you deserve what you want. Having enough self-respect to walk away when your boundaries and standards are being compromised is difficult, but in the end it will lead you to a fulfilling relationship.

chapter 5

Bumps in the Dating Road:
Readiness, Rejection, Recycling,
Rebounding, Retreating

The five Rs—readiness, rejection, recycling, rebounding, retreating—are common bumps in the road that you may or may not experience. Encountering one may make you feel like a failure, but that is not the case. You are trying to figure out what you want, where you're going and who—if anyone—is going with you. Despite all your hard work and optimism, the dating landscape can be tough to navigate, but even tougher if you are unprepared for mishaps, missteps, and mistakes. Many things can happen that are frustrating and upsetting, some caused by the person you are considering for a date, and some originating within yourself. There are five questions to ask yourself before you go back out there, and five experiences that can send you scurrying back to the safe not-dating place. Everyone experiences one or more of the five Rs. Knowing that it's normal and okay will make the dating experience easier for you. The five Rs are:

1. **Readiness:** Don't force yourself out into the world before you are ready. It's okay to try dating if an opportunity comes along and you haven't really thought about it yet, but it's helpful to make a proactive and conscious decision that you are ready to date. Further, you want to have an idea of what kind of dating experience you are ready for at this moment. A short-lived fling may be fun and require little emotional involvement, but choosing a mate for that is very different from looking for a life partner. Therefore, it's not just important to know that you are ready but to know *what* you are ready for at this time.

2. **Rejection:** Know that you will both reject and be rejected. Don't take it personally. Be sure to toughen up before you put yourself in a position to be scrutinized and then rejected. Your affirmations are still important, and taking a new view of rejection as something that is beneficial is important. A continuing mantra must be, "I only want to be with people who want to be with me."

3. **Recycling:** This is a feeling of being thrust, without warning, back into the pit of grief and despair

over your breakup. Many times recycling is triggered by dating because it signals that you are moving on and some part of you doesn't want to do that. You may feel emptiness instead of the jubilation you expected. When you feel empty and drained, you can be pulled anew down the rabbit hole of grief. Suddenly you feel as if you just broke up yesterday and all the emotions of loss come flooding in. This can happen with or without dating, but dating can be a trigger.

4. **Rebounding:** This means going into another relationship right out of the old one without working through a breakup. Sometimes a rebound is a response not just to a breakup but to your ex moving on quickly. It is possible but not probable that your rebound relationship can work. Even if it does, you may have emotional issues connected to unresolved issues from your breakup. Try to see a rebound for what it is: a temporary fix on the way to permanent healing. If you stay in a rebound, you may find yourself narrowing your ability to be emotionally available to others, not just your partner but friends and family as well. Try to use a rebound as a pit stop and not a final destination.

5. **Retreating:** This means moving back to the cocoon that you left to peek outside and see what was happening. Someone may have convinced you that it's time, but you feel unsure. Without clear knowledge

of what phase of healing your head and heart are in, you may just rush back out there without a clear idea of whether or not you're ready to date. Even if you feel ready, you may fall apart when you get there, discover that your skin is still very thin, and that you are susceptible to being hurt over anything and everything. Another reason for retreat is attracting the wrong kind of date right away. Sometimes a recycle turns into a retreat. Some retreats are brief while others take longer because you're not ready, but you also discover you have work to do and need to get centered before you take the plunge.

Readiness

Christie, 33 / I don't know when I'm ready or what it is I'm ready for. Of course I would love to meet Mr. Right and fall in love but the thing is that although I'd love that, I'm not ready for it. Still, I'd like to be seeing someone or even dating occasionally. I am not sure what it is I want.

Troy, 26 / I'm sure that I'm ready but when I put my profile on dating websites or agree to setups by friends, I pull back. I can't seem to figure out, from one minute to the next, what I want.

Robert, 35 / I know I'm ready for a relationship but when I bring that up on early dates, it seems to scare

people away. I know what I want and that I'm willing
to put those cards on the table and not waste my time
or someone else's time, but that seems to scare people!

Tamara, 42 / I think I'm ready but then an opportunity
to date comes along and I run away. Am I truly not
ready or just afraid of being hurt again? I can't seem to
tell the difference.

After you've gone through a major breakup and a time of healing, you start to think about going back out there. Even if you
haven't thought about it, people in your life may be prompting
you to start dating again. Some think that getting right back out
there is essential, but that's usually not the case. You need time
to grieve, rebuild your life, and regain your self-confidence. This
is done on your timetable and no one else's.

How much time does it take to get over a relationship? Let
me assure you that any formula you've heard is wrong. One I've
heard is that getting over a relationship takes half as long as the
relationship lasted. I have clients who were married twenty years
or more and if I told them they needed ten years to recover,
they'd be jumping off the nearest bridge. Every breakup is different, people handle breakups in different ways, and there's no one
time frame that fits all. You cannot paint breakups with a broad
brush, and no one formula could possibly apply to all people.

Everyone knows someone who flies from one relationship
to the next, never feeling pain and perhaps even managing to be
friends with the ex. Everyone knows someone who continues to
feel bitter over a long-ago breakup. The time it takes you to get

over it depends on you, your ego strength, your support system, the work you put into it, and other factors that are unique to you and your situation. People who encourage you to get right back out there and forget the ex ever existed are unhelpful. If you try to deny your past, you'll never learn from it. So ignore harmful advice, strange formulations, and people who "mean well."

If others are pushing you too quickly, set a boundary with them, being careful to construct your statement with "I" language, for example, "I appreciate your care and concern, but for right now, I'm not ready yet. When I am, I will let you know." Depending on the person and your relationship, you may need to enforce a boundary and simply repeat what you've said. Some well-meaning friends and family may push that it's already been weeks or months, and you should be ready by now, but arguing the point will get you nowhere, so simply repeat that you're not ready.

Pressure can also come from within yourself. While you may want to be honest and true to yourself, you may not be able to ascertain your own state of readiness. As my client quoted above said, it can be challenging to figure out the difference between not being ready because you're still working through things from your last relationship and fear of being hurt. It usually feels the same. However, there are a few things you can do to decide.

What Are You Ready For?

The first order of business is to decide what you're ready for. A client was clear she wanted to be married and have children, but she had been in a relationship with someone who had promised those things but couldn't deliver. She started dating about a year after the breakup but was practically having a tantrum after every date. Her impatience with the process was clear because she wasn't finding Mr. Wonderful Enough to Be the Father of My Future Children.

When you've been in a long-term relationship and then out of one for some time, you want the dating period to be short as possible. The trouble is that you rush headlong into a relationship just to avoid more dating. "I don't want to spend a lot of time dating" is no reason to get into a relationship. In fact, you are probably not ready for one. Being ready can imply many things. Being ready to date or to put yourself out there doesn't necessarily mean you're ready for a long-term commitment or marriage and children, even if that is what you eventually want to happen. Being ready may not mean that you're up for more than "looking and considering." Because being ready means different things to different people, and the first question to ask is, *What does it mean to me at this particular time?* Your answer to this question can, and should, evolve over time. You may desperately want to have a family and put it on your list of nonnegotiables for your forever partner. However, it's not a good idea to reject people at the outset just because they do not seem to be family material. Put your permanent plans in your back pocket for now and allow yourself to get comfortable with the idea of being with a new someone rather than scrutinizing every first date for co-parenting potential. Remember, hungry people make poor shoppers.

Where to Shop and How to Shop

Several of my clients who are well past their breakup still fear dating. They rehearse the possible pitfalls and ask themselves, "What if no one wants me?" These disaster scenarios are counterproductive. Once we work through that, the next question is usually, "Where do I meet someone?" The question comes from old and young, straight and gay, newly single after a long marriage, and those who were in a short-lived whirlwind romance.

Part of moving on from a breakup is building a new life. Nothing is as attractive as someone who has a full life and many interests and hobbies. I always suggest that my clients take classes, join professional organizations, take up new hobbies, and seek out opportunities to meet new people—get out and mingle. You never know what will happen. You do know what will happen if you stay home: nothing.

Consider Meetup.com groups as well as social groups based in communities or places of worship. One client met her husband while planting a community garden and another met his wife in a sunrise exercise class. Again, these activities will get you out and about and help you figure out what you like and what people you like being around. One client signed up for a class that he thought would be interesting but found his fellow classmates to be standoffish and opinionated. He lost interest in the class because there were group projects and class discussion and he felt tortured being with these people. He wanted a different group and it took him awhile, but he found ones that he enjoyed.

If you go to events, you may make friends who invite you to other events and your circle of friends widens. As your circle widens, so does the number of people you come into contact with. Someone who knows someone who knows someone may be your forever love. A client met her fiancé through a women's social group she joined when she "swore off men." She made friends with several of the women and they enjoyed outings and traveled together. A year after she joined the group, she was invited to a barbecue where she was introduced to her friend's cousin. There was an instant connection, they dated, and eventually they became engaged. It's not paramount that you be ready to date before you start widening your circles; in fact it's probably better that you're not. It's also not the end of your dating life if you join up with a group that excludes the gender of the people you normally date. As your circles widen and the number of activities you engage in grows, so do your chances of meeting someone you may be interested in romantically. Healthy people are attracted to others who have a wide range of interests, and having them not only increases your chances and your choices of meeting a healthy partner, but makes you more attractive.

Online Dating: Welcome to a Brave New World

If your social circles and activities are not working or you are too busy to put a lot of time into them, you may want to try online dating. There are many dating sites and many success stories from those dating sites. Because so many work long hours or have joint custody of their children, it's become commonplace and does not carry the social stigma it did just a few short years ago.

Don't scoff at online dating if you've never tried it, but don't throw yourself into it before examining the ins and outs of it, especially if you don't know anyone who has done it or don't know what to expect from it. There are books and articles about online dating and if it's new to you, or you're coming out of a long-term relationship, it's time to do some research before taking the plunge. If you do your homework, you can avoid some of the pitfalls and problems unique to online dating.

Putting yourself on a dating site and meeting new people is a completely new concept for many people. How do you go from strictly terrestrial meetings to online dating? Well, it's not easy. While some jump in optimistically, others quake with fear at the thought. How do you know who is telling the truth and who is not? How do you define who you are in a few short words in a profile? How do you tell the people looking to hook up from those looking for a relationship?

First, be advised that there are mostly normal and decent people on dating sites. However, con men and women do exist and do troll. There are reasons why almost every site says not to communicate with someone via personal email; stick to the dating site email. People lie about age, weight, and marital status, and post phony photographs. Balance interest with a healthy dose of skepticism. If a person says, "I'm not on here a lot so email me at this address," that is usually a red flag. Some con artists zero in on people they think are naïve, such as those in their early twenties or those over fifty. They will explain the lack of a photo with some excuse such as their computer won't upload it or some other technical glitch. Do not talk to anyone without a photo; someone who sounds too good to be true probably is. It's easy to run web searches, and some people pay for a background search. Be careful of those services as well and research the software company before plunking down hard-earned money for information you can find yourself.

After you've done some due diligence on potential dates, you may fall into the trap of communicating solely by electronic means. Both text and email can create a version of a person in your mind that doesn't really exist. Many interpret written communication as what they want to hear and ignore anything that doesn't support their view of their new friend. Avoid the temptation to spend too much time in text and email. Be sure to limit your electronic conversations and spend time talking on the phone and seeing someone in person.

Try not to take things too personally. This is extra important in online dating. Some people are only willing to explore opportunities that seem to have a real chance at working out. Others enjoy meeting many people without being clear as to what they are looking for. Each person's agenda is different and most have absolutely nothing to do with you. Therefore it is imperative you remain clear on who you are and what your value is, and don't let another person's disinterest affect you negatively. Most likely, it has nothing to do with you. Being rejected does not necessarily mean you do not measure up as a person. Take the rejection as a cue that getting involved would be bad for both of you, but the other person got the clue first. Be grateful that someone is not willing to waste your time. While some people may find online dating easier than others, don't allow a difficult time to discourage you. Use your affirmations as a way to keep your perspective and enforce your self-esteem.

I have reviewed client online dating profiles and found some to be wordy and others to hardly say anything. I usually suggest that you start off with the type of people you like to be around such as, "I like smart, interesting people with a good sense of humor and a desire to travel and try new things." If you are not the type of person who wants to travel or try new things and consider yourself a homebody, make sure you frame that as well. Several of my clients like to relax after a long work week. "I feel so boring when I can't think of a single extracurricular activity that I really like to do." You can write, "I like people who don't take life too seriously, don't have to fill every free second with a thrill or an adventure, and can enjoy a weekend at home cooking together and watching movies." Although your first paragraph works best if it's upbeat and positive, you may include what is unacceptable to you. Couch it in positive words, "I try not to judge and to each his or her own, but I have trouble with people who [hunt, argue politics, exist solely on fast food, are vegan]." This will ferret out those who are a definite "no, just no" for you.

Then talk about yourself in the next paragraph, "I'm a bit shy, but once you get to know me, I open up. I'm honest and caring and friends say I have a good sense of humor and am fun to be around. I'll try new things that don't involve eating exotic foods or falling from heights (no parachutes)." Or "I'm outgoing and love to meet new people. I like to try challenging things that I've never done before like bungee jumping. My dream is to go to Tahiti one day." Try to inject your personality into your comments. You can mention your job but don't mention that you are well-to-do or happily impoverished. Both can be a signal to the wrong people.

Finally, wrap it up with your idea of a first date, for example, "First dates can be unnerving for everyone! Let's meet for coffee or lunch and if things go well, we can collaborate on a great second date. My suggestions might be going to a museum or checking out the new rock climbing wall at the mall." Go light and easy on the first date and for the second date, suggest something cerebral as well as something not so cerebral. Be sure that your first two dates are in public and preferably in the daytime.

The best profiles are concise but explain something about who you are, what you like to do, and what kind of people you like to be around. Show your profile to your friends and ask if it really conveys who you are. Post photographs that show the real you doing real things. Avoid selfies and mirror shots. While you may need to update your photos to make them recent, ask friends or family to snap photos of you when you're unaware they're doing so. No, you don't want the one that shows you spilling something all over yourself or the one where you are frowning, but you can flip through them to get two or three candid shots that capture the essence of who you are. Since we are usually terrible judges of our own photos, ask friends which ones they like and which ones are "worth a thousand words." The best photos of you and the ones that show who you really are may not be the same, so a mix of the two is best.

Online dating can be fun and challenging, but you're ready to go because you have your "even though" statements, your self-esteem is strong, and you know that you only want to be with people who want to be with you. Online dating can be a great adventure, and you may well find the person who is right for you. When you launch your single self into cyberspace, chances are you will meet wonderful people you would never have met otherwise. Have fun, be safe, and remember who you are and what you are worth.

You've Shopped; Now What?

The early dates should be about testing the waters, seeing how you feel, and trying to have fun. If you take things too seriously, you're going to look at everyone through a warped filter. Many times the person who could turn into a terrific mate does not make a good first impression. Unless there is something obviously troubling about your date, be more fun and less scrutinizing. No one says you have to get married after dessert. Learn how to enjoy another person's company with no expectations. You will be surprised how that small attitude adjustment can help. Maybe this isn't your future co-parent or someone you'll introduce to family and friends, but for now this is someone worth sharing a brief period with, so try to make it as nice as you can for both of you. You are likely not ready for more at this time and that's okay.

Bear in mind that it's hard to gauge in the first week, month, or even six months if this person is "the one." Further, you don't have to know. What you need to know is that no matter what happens, you will be okay. Make that an affirmation and say it every day. If you keep that attitude throughout dating and even in the beginning of a relationship, you will do just fine.

Picking people to go out with can have good, bad, or catastrophic results. No one wears a T-shirt that announces what they want now or in the future. You may really like someone and seem to click and then the bombshell drops that this person is not on the same page as you when it comes to the future. While some people find it disconcerting to be asked, "So what are you looking for?" on a first date, others welcome the question. It is a fairly personal and intimate question, and if you are uncomfortable with it, I suggest saying, "Well, I'd like to be in a relationship again, but for now I'm open to meeting people and becoming comfortable. What about you?" One thing to keep in mind is that even people who say they want a committed relationship may not know that isn't what they really want. Most people who have a series of relationship failures will rarely entertain the notion that intimacy really scares them or that maybe they have a problem with commitment. Others may be aware of it but aren't going to hang it as a sign around their neck to announce that if you want someone with issues, this is your guy or gal.

Some people are on dating sites to do some light dating, getting to know people, and having something to do on a Saturday night. I once asked a client if he had any hobbies. He said, "Yes, of course. Dating is my hobby." He had some desire for a long-term relationship but said, "It's a numbers game. You have to meet as many as possible to find that person." Another client agreed to exclusivity with someone she really liked and he seemed to like her, but after a few weeks, she back-pedaled a bit wondering if there were mates more suitable than he. This was perplexing to me because she hated first dates and the person she was seeing was treating her very well and acting like a good and honest person. We explored it further and while she maintained she really wanted a committed relationship, something was scaring her and causing her to back away from anyone who had the potential to be a long-term partner. After a few months of working on her inventories, it seemed clear that she was afraid of intimacy due to some issues with her unavailable father. So there may be times when you question your readiness at every stage, but that's a good thing. Don't doubt yourself; think of it as double-checking.

The problem is that most people are out there to "see what happens," thinking that is the wrong approach when it's not. While there are people on the dating scene who are going to reject possible mates outright if the connection doesn't feel strong in the beginning, most people would be better off to take a "whatever happens, happens" attitude. If you want a committed relationship, of course you're going to stay away from people who are using dating sites as a revolving bedroom door. However, you can give chances to those who are "open to possibilities," which reflects a healthy attitude. Being open to investing some time and energy will take you further than just wringing your hands and whining, "I don't know!" Taking a calm, smooth approach is important and—once again—your "I'll be okay no matter what" mantra is the key to success.

Rejection

Marianne, 46 / It seemed like every person I talked to, on an Internet dating site, would eventually get to the point that they no longer wanted to talk. I saved most of the messages to examine them for clues as to what I could possibly be doing wrong. I spend days going over them and it seemed no matter what approach I took, it didn't work.

Jenna, 38 / I had no problem getting a first date, but I either didn't get a second date or third. I started to ask, at the end of each date, what their plans were, and if it didn't include another date, why was that? Most people are very uncomfortable with that question, but I said I'm an intelligent, caring woman with a good sense of humor so you're not going to destroy me if you're honest. Most of their feedback had nothing to do with me. Except in one instance where the man had lied on his profile about being legally divorced, and realized after meeting me that I was going to figure that out and not want to get involved with him.

Tom, 33 / Every woman I met via online dating seemed
to expect a suave, sophisticated Wall Street banker
when we met. Yes, I work on Wall Street. Yes, I'm a
banker. But when I come home, I want to relax, go
to a place where I can wear jeans and a button down
shirt. Everyone seemed disappointed I wasn't my job
and wasn't taking them to dinner at the most expensive
restaurants in the city. If we were headed to coupledom,
I'd be different and spend more money but online
dating is an expensive endeavor for a guy and I can't
afford to take every woman out on the town on every
date. We went to nice places, but not upscale, and I
rarely got a second date.

When you get feedback that someone is not interested in a second or third date, your brain immediately goes to rejection land and refuses to come back. It sits in the corner and feels sorry that no one will ever love you because you were rejected by someone you weren't even sure you liked. Preparing for possible rejection means incorporating affirmations or "even though" statements into your daily routine. Examples of these are:

I only want to be with people who want to be with me.
Even though X is not interested in a second date, I'm still
    attractive, personable, and worthwhile.
I am a person of choice, not convenience.
Even though this relationship did not work, I am lovable.

The right person will find time for me and our relationship.
I will feel secure in the right relationship at the right time.

When you experience rejection, keep your standards high. If you want just anyone, you'll find someone out there just looking for a pulse. You want someone who also has high standards and whose standards happen to fit with who you are and what you are all about. A recent blog reader talked of giving herself a year before she began dating after a big breakup. She was self-assured and confident, and had built her own life. Almost as soon as she got back out there, she met a guy and they clicked. He whispered sweet nothings to her and she loved it. He was still sweet-talking until the day he confessed that he had been seeing another woman as well as her. The other woman wanted him to choose—and he chose her.

She had no idea he was seeing someone else and was devastated by the news and felt "back to square one." Although she hadn't had the year of healing, it felt that way to her. It's tempting to jump in after you've given yourself time to heal and grow, but sometimes you miss things or assume things that may or may not be true. Too often those returning to dating want the very next person to be the one, and they miss information that is necessary to understanding that the new person is not the one.

Another pitfall is to give yourself time, work really hard on being ready, and then fail to realize that it's still possible to choose wrong or not have enough information to make a good decision. Getting through a breakup, working through grief and underlying issues, and building your self-esteem is challenging.

The payoff is that you are now in a healthier place than ever before. But even the healthiest people can have false starts and dashed hopes. Don't think that your work has been in vain or that you're never going to meet someone if the first few experiences don't pan out. While it's hard to have to pull back "yet again," know that you're growing and changing and will meet a compatible partner.

Sometimes it's not you at all but someone who is approaching dating the wrong way while seeming to be a great choice. One of my clients says he looks for certain types and will mull over a profile and then send a brief message. He will message twenty or thirty women and maybe get back one or two replies. Like a client I mentioned earlier, he too believes it is a numbers game. Although he's actively dating, he admits that he's not sure if he's "in it to win it" or even what he wants, but he likes to try to beat the odds. Sometimes when he's out with women, he's sent so many messages, he's not even sure who she is or why she piqued his interest. He's handsome and well-spoken and probably charms the women he dates. What she has no way of figuring out is that he has no idea what he wants. When they part at the end of the first date, she probably assumes she's going to hear from him again and when she doesn't, may wonder what she said or did that was wrong. If you have that experience, don't instantly think it's something about you, since you have no idea what is going on with your date. Avoid the temptation to examine what you wore, said, did or did not do. It may have nothing to do with you and everything to do with the other person.

If you find yourself going out on first dates but rarely getting to a second or third date or having a series of short-lived relationships, don't fall into the trap of projecting the worst-case scenario of being alone forever. If you allow that negative thinking to creep in, you may start to lower your standards or present yourself as someone you're not. If you're not feeling good about yourself, don't try to reverse all the hard work you've done. Healthy people want to be with other healthy people. The closer you get to the healthy pool, the fewer fish are swimming around but the ones that are swimming around are good fish and they do exist. Don't let a bad run spoil your outlook or cause you to forget your goal of not just having a relationship, but having a good one.

When you enter the world of dating, you accept being judged by another person. If you accept a date, you're making a kind of emotional commitment. If you're going on your third or fourth date, you likely have some idea if you want to be in or out. If you decide you want to be in and the other person decides to be out, you're going to experience a bit of pain. Many of my clients are perplexed when another does not act in congruence with expected norms of rational behavior. They don't expect to be rejected after having three or four wonderful dates. If you are ready to explore the idea of an exclusive relationship with someone you think is really great, it can be a loud thud when you fall back to earth because your new friend doesn't see a future and is moving on. Remember that you want to be with people who want to be with you. Don't spend time trying to analyze the behavior of a person who has suddenly switched off; there are people out there who are right for you.

People who are rejecting you don't really know you anymore than the ones you are rejecting. Don't take it to heart when someone who hardly knows you rejects you. Even if you feel a connection or a spark or can see a real future, your date must see the same thing. Otherwise, there is no use in it. There is nothing wrong with you if someone does not see the future you see. There are plenty of people rejecting perfectly wonderful people because they are not where they need to be to accept a wonderful person in a chaotic life. One woman reports, "I had a friend whose cousin was moving back to the area and thought we would be 'perfect' for each other. He had been divorced awhile and had a five-year-old son. I had two kids around the same age. We worked in the same field and had a lot of the same hobbies, including reading and love for classics, movies, books, art, and so on. She showed us photos of each other and we both agreed to meet, but we had trouble making our schedules mesh for a while." They spoke on the phone almost every night, discussed books, movies, television, and the like. He read books that no one had heard of—and she read the same ones. There were so many "me too" moments when it came to unusual things. As she readied for her first date, she felt as if she already knew him and the date was just a formality since they had talked so much. She described it as if she was going to meet an old friend instead of a potential love interest for the first time.

Even though she assumed they were going to be a done deal, she wore a skirt, heels, and a nice silk blouse. Normally not a skirt and heels person, she enjoyed dressing up for dates. As she drove to the restaurant, she presumed they would be a couple by the end of the evening. When she arrived at the restaurant and spotted him sitting at the bar, he was wearing jeans, work boots, and a dress shirt. He noticed her and waved her over. At first she felt a bit put off by the wave, thinking it would have been more polite to come over and greet her. Still, she excused it on the basis that the bar was crowded and he might not get the seat back. She walked over, they said hello in a warm and friendly tone. He gave her a brief half hug but continued to sit on the stool, never offering her the seat and telling her, "Our table should be ready in about ten minutes."

At first they were a bit uneasy, but they soon picked up the tempo they had on the phone and all seemed fine. He was polite, funny, and recalled different things she had said, which made her feel good. When the waiter asked if they'd like dessert, he didn't ask her but said, "No, we're fine, just the check." She didn't let her disappointment show and they continued easy banter for the next few minutes. On the way out of the restaurant, he put his hand in the small of her back, a gesture she found charming. They got outside and he said, "Where are you parked?" She pointed to the left. He pointed to the right and said, "I'm over there, so I guess we'll part here. Nice meeting you!" and he took off. She stood there dumbfounded.

Not only had the evening been very different from what she expected, but she knew she was never going to hear from him again. On Monday, her friend confirmed that suspicion. "He said you live too far." *Live too far?* He knew where she lived when they agreed to the date. She didn't buy it and pressed her friend a bit more. The friend shrugged and said, "He's funny sometimes.

It's hard to tell what's really going on with him." With more pressure her friend finally said, "He also thought you were over-dressed for a pub setting." Overdressed? How did that translate to rejection? He thought her outfit was indicative of trying too hard. It turned him off.

She felt rejected as if there was something wrong with her. She had told some of her friends about him over the weeks they talked on the phone and they had asked her what happened, but she didn't want to talk about it. When she finally opened up to a friend, she said, "If he had been totally into you and wanted to have a second date with you, wouldn't you have been talking about the fact he didn't get up to greet you or offer you the seat?" She thought about it and supposed she would have. "Even if he wasn't interested in a second date, your car was parked at the far end of a parking lot, couldn't he have walked you there? He didn't check with you to see if you wanted dessert; he decided it was time to go." Even though those things seemed to suggest he was something of a jerk, she was overwhelmed with feelings of rejection.

Their many weeks of wonderful conversation were eclipsed by the fact that she was overdressed? It did not compute. Of course it didn't because she valued the conversation and the "click" more than he did. She could not imagine rejecting him even if he had shown up in a tuxedo. The excuse about the dis-tance was illogical since they knew it from the first minute they started talking. She didn't get it, but she didn't have to. If some-thing like this happens to you, your inability to "get it" means that you are a nicer and more logical person than the "jerk" who is holding you to ridiculous standards. It means you're not ridiculous and that is why you can't wrap your head around it. It's important to give yourself credit here, not blame yourself for not meeting someone's preposterous criteria.

When a person rejects you, many times that's all you can think about. A client complained that men who were beneath her were rejecting her and she could only focus on that. In reality she would have rejected them eventually anyway and they might have picked up on it. To the man who thought all women wanted him because he was a banker, I suggested he take that off his profile. As soon as he did, he met more down-to-earth women who enjoyed a lunch out or an inexpensive dinner.

The point is that what you are calling rejection is simply someone making a decision that the two of you have no future. Whether it is you or your date making the decision, the decision is being made. A woman I mentioned above was not making it to second or third dates. Why? It could have been something in her online dating profile; it could have been the men she was choosing. It could have been not spending time getting to know someone before the date. It could have been that she wasn't ready to date and was sending out that vibe to her dates.

Another possibility that people don't consider is that "water seeks its own level." Your partner reflects your level of emotional health, but so do the people who come before. The person you are having a date with could be a user, a player, a deceiver. You may be giving off the vibe that you aren't playing in that sandbox anymore. Perhaps you are being rejected because you're too healthy for some. Almost no one I suggest this to wants to hear it, but it's true. A man came to see me one time and said, "From the moment I met her I knew she was having none of my 'disappearing act' [he tended to go along until the fourth or fifth month and then vanished for a while claiming to need space]. I almost didn't ask her on a second date because I had a strong feeling that she would not be there when I got back from one of my excursions." He wasn't ready and there was no woman in the world who was going to make him ready, although many had tried. But this woman was not going to play his "come-here-go-away" game. With a bit of sadness he said, "I don't think I've ever been in the position to *reject* a woman. Normally I screw around so much that they just throw me out and I'm on to another one. I actually rejected this one because I could tell, from the first night we met, she was too confident and secure to wait around for me to come back from my 'me time.' As much as I could leave women, I couldn't have one say, 'Fine, go and don't come back.' And I know that's exactly the type she was."

Therefore, what many call "rejection" is anything but. It typically has more to do with them than with you. People scurry away from dating, or even meeting, because they're not ready for you or they have issues that you don't want to deal with anyway. However, if they are the first to pull away, you're the one who feels rejected. If you're lowering your standards and are still being rejected, you start to think, "How much lower can I go?" However, it's not about lowering standards or trying to figure out rejection. It's about powering through so-called rejection and moving along to find the one you really should be with.

I've heard so many stories from people about being rejected by dates and, like the guy who didn't give up his bar stool, I remark, "You realize that this person sounds like a complete idiot [or a jerk or a few other choice words]." On the *GPYB* blog we forgo the choice words and use the term "bananahead," which my readers have shortened to "BH." Many will say, "Yes, but *even* the bananaheads don't want me." This is not about trying to make the BHs of the world like you. They don't like you because you are not one of them. I know plenty of men like the one above who said to me, straight out, "She's not going to put up with my BS." If you have raised your self-esteem and have built a new and wonderful life, you are clearly a person of worth. Someone looking for a victim or playing games is not going to give you a second glance. Because "water seeks its own level," there is a very distinct possibility that people are not going to like you because you are too healthy for them.

You don't need the whole world panting after you and wishing you were with them. Don't think you need to be richer, smarter, more worldly, better looking. Good-looking people often fear that others are attracted to them solely for their looks. Well-to-do people often fear that others are attracted to them solely for their money. No matter who you are or what you do or what you look like, there will always be some question as to why someone is with you and why someone doesn't want to be with you. If you're going out on the dating scene, experiencing rejection is part of the package.

It can be deflating when you like someone who doesn't like you, but the right partner will see it the same way you see it.

You don't want to be dragging people into relationships—and you don't want to spend time trying to convince someone to be with you who doesn't want to. It's the same thing with someone who doesn't want to continue after the first date. It doesn't feel great when your hopes are dashed and daydreams crumble, but finding the right person is about finding someone who wants to be with you as much as you want to be with them. Don't take rejection personally; it is a sign that you've dodged a bullet.

Recycling

> **Steve, 31 /** I thought I was over my ex, but every date made me want him more and more. I would come home from a date and all I could think of was my ex. When I was with someone I really liked and who liked me, we would date awhile but the comparisons to my ex would get worse and not better. It doomed all possibilities of a relationship.

> **Brian, 33 /** I didn't date until over a year after our breakup. My ex had been with someone for several months. I wanted to be ready and I wanted to feel free and happy on dates, but I came home miserable. So many times I was tempted to call her up and say, "Who are we kidding? We should be together, not with these other people." But she had moved on and would have thought I was crazy.

Barbara, 49 / I started to recycle when I really felt myself letting go of my ex but had not found anyone new yet. I recycled when I got to the healed place I thought I wanted to be and found "no there there."

"Recycling" happens when you are feeling better and you think you are making progress, and then suddenly you're miserable again. It happens whether you're dating or not dating. It's part of the process. You think you're making good progress and then all of a sudden you are buried deep in an emotional hole. It's very common to recycle around an anniversary or the ex's birthday or your own birthday. There are times when it hits unexpectedly for no apparent reason. However, it seems to feel worse and more painful when it happens after you've started dating again. Dating is supposed to be about "moving on," but here the ex is in your thoughts and your dreams, and you feel terrible, all over again, about the breakup.

If you're pining for your ex, you are most likely missing the familiarity that does not exist on a first date. If you didn't initiate the breakup, you may curse the fact that you're on the dating scene again. You may fall into the trap of idealizing your ex, thinking the relationship might have worked and you could have avoided this scenario, where you sit sobbing in your car after what was a decent night out. If it was a dreadful night out, the pining for (or anger at) your ex may be even more intense. However, it is not your ex that you are missing; it's the comfort that you can't find when you are just getting to know another person.

The last thing you want to feel after a date is longing for your ex. You have given dating a lot of thought. You have tried hard to convince yourself that someone—better than your ex—is out there for you and will want you as much you want them. You can be with someone you've known for some time or someone you are meeting for the first time or someone you've been seeing a lot and then, out of the blue, you're recycling. Sometimes it begins with a dream; other times it can begin with a random thought or the fact that you almost called your new person by your ex's name.

Recycling is a part of the grief process and can happen days, months, or even years after you thought you were over it. It happens whether you're with or not with someone else. Recycling occurs when unpredictable remnants of grief show up at inopportune times. One client said, "I was with someone who had a breakdown. His best friend was killed in a car wreck while he was another passenger in the car. For a year, he couldn't deal with his grief, guilt, and depression. Being a good girlfriend, and knowing how well things worked for us, I stayed that year and tried to pull him through. Nothing worked. Then he started to break down. He stayed out late, was fired from his job, moved home with his parents, and didn't want to see me much. Then one day he told me he couldn't be in a relationship. I grieved for a long time for the person he was, and the relationship we had before the accident. It was hard. About two years after our breakup, I started dating again. I met a lot of nice guys but wanted to understand the 'lay of the land,' so to speak, before dating seriously. I was on my fourth or fifth date since joining the dating service and everyone seemed nice and friendly. Then one night I went home and started to feel guilt and remorse about the fact that I just left my ex in his time of need. None of it made sense since he broke up with me. But I felt as if I was losing my mind. I wanted him back in the worst way. I almost called him. It was very difficult not to do that. I stayed off the dating site for a while, did my grief work yet again, and looked at some of the residual anger and hurt I could not get rid of previously."

Sometimes, recycling doesn't mean a thing, and sometimes it's a sign you still have work to do that you may not know about yet. The woman made the right decision to not call her ex, but she had guilt about leaving him "in his time of need." Many have the same kind of guilt. Even if the ex initiated the breakup, if later the ex lost a job or got sick, some feel they should have insisted on staying and hanging on. But love is not about sacrificing yourself for the sake of someone who doesn't want you around. These residual recycling episodes may be a night of crying over your ex and then letting it go, or it may be a sign that you have more work to do on your breakup. Either way, it's not weakness or anything that you're doing wrong. It happens when you're dating and when you're not. It's a part of the grief process and you don't have to spend a lot of time worrying about it. Don't let a bit of recycling throw you so far off course it makes you afraid to get out there again.

The newness of dating and unfamiliar people can make you want to run back into the arms of someone familiar. One woman, who had been broken up almost two years, had been with her new boyfriend about two months when she felt herself ready to burst into tears as they were making love. She was suddenly overcome with thoughts of her ex and how tender he was, not that her new boyfriend wasn't, but he was in a different way. When her boyfriend took note of her impending tears, she said she was getting her period and he asked if she wanted to stop. She did and he just lay there holding her and telling her it was going to be okay. She felt even more guilt that she had done that, but she didn't experience it again and it faded. It would not have been good form to tell her boyfriend that she was thinking of her ex. Sparing both of them from what could have been an ugly night, she worked through it and in the morning they made love. She was truly present and felt closer to her new boyfriend than ever.

Recycling can even make you want to run back to the loneliness and the boredom of your old relationship. Pining for a relationship that didn't work can make you very nervous and very upset. It usually happens because you're doing something new and different or because there is some residual grief that needs to express itself. Either way, recycling can happen unexpectedly and make you feel unhinged. But work through it as a temporary state and nothing to change your new life over or worse, try to run back to your old one.

Rebounding

Maura, 38 / My ex moved in with someone almost two weeks after we broke up. This guy said he'd be with every woman on the East Coast when his best friend divorced. No, he just went with a woman that he had nothing good to say about before that time. I started seeing someone about a month later and that month seemed like the longest time. I didn't want to be rebounding and I rebounded myself into a relationship that took from me emotionally, physically, and financially. When you're rebounding, you've lost all perspective.

Trevor, 31 / Enough time had gone on, or so I thought, but my ex kept calling and my very patient new girlfriend was growing tired of it. When she gave me an ultimatum, I made the wrong choice. I chose the ex. After that didn't work (for like the fifth time), I tried to talk to the other woman and she wouldn't have anything to do with me. She said, "I was your rebound once; I won't be it again." Next time I was sure I was over someone before I started seeing someone again.

It is always hard to know if you're rebounding, even if enough time has passed to think that you're not. It's hard to know if you're getting involved with people who are rebounding. Many are unsure if they're over their ex or if their ex is over them. Many are unsure if someone has started dating because the ex is dating. Sometimes no one seems to know.

Sometimes rebounding is a response to "my ex found someone new so I have to do it too." Sometimes it's about feeling attractive without a need to get into a relationship. You can go out and garner attention without dragging someone else through your emotional mud. Both men and women use others to feel attractive again, but one woman summed it up nicely: "My relationship was so rocky for so long I had stopped caring about my looks. I went to get a haircut and the stylist talked me into highlights that looked great. I lost some weight and started taking care of my skin. The first few nights out, I should have been okay with just attracting attention from guys, but no, I had to start dating one. A rebound wasn't fair to him. I did have a bad relationship but that was no excuse to hurt someone." When you are being flirty and fun, it's one thing, but don't lead someone down a path you're not yet ready to go.

It's also important to know how long someone has been away from an ex before making a decision to see someone. You want to know if the person has spent any time alone during the time between the big breakup and now. One man told me, "I'd had a few girlfriends, mostly meaningless, and was not still over my ex when I started to see a woman I was friends with and truly cared about. All was good in the beginning, but when things got rocky, I definitely projected my ex onto her and started to express a lot of anger at her that I never had at my ex. We were headed for the end, when I was going through some papers one day and I found a photo of my ex. Astonishingly, I thought it was a photo of my current girlfriend when I looked at it quickly. I never thought about how closely they resembled each other. It was clear I was not only on the rebound, but treating my current girlfriend the way I wished I had responded to my ex in the final days of the relationship. Unfortunately my girlfriend was done with me by that time, and I was never able to repair it."

He had never really completed the work he needed to do, especially the needed anger work between serious girlfriends. He had a series of less important relationships so when he met the second woman, he was sure he was over the first. He hadn't even made the connection between the first and second until he saw the photograph. How did he not see how similar they looked? "Well, my first girlfriend wore her hair up a lot but my second girlfriend didn't. The photo I found was of my first girlfriend with her hair down and that is when I made the connection. I didn't go out with the second because she looked like the first, but I'm sure there was some kind of connection."

Just because time has passed does not mean you're *not* on the rebound. If you've filled your time with going out a lot, that doesn't mean that when you do become serious about someone that you're not still in rebound. It's important to make sure you've worked through the hurt and anger. Sometimes people know they're on the rebound. Since you shouldn't string someone along, it's good to admit that you've broken off a major relationship and try to be as honest as you can about where you are. Being on the rebound and not being truthful about it, to yourself or others, can lead to many hurt feelings.

"Keeping your side of the street clean" is something that I introduced in *GPYB* and is very important in dating. It's a fine line to walk sometimes, because it's not always clear where you are. But if you have an inkling that you're rebounding, try to be as honest as possible and try not to hurt someone else. You don't have to come out and say, "Guess what? I'm on the rebound so don't get too attached!" However, it's good to keep expectations at a certain level for you both. If things change that is fine, but keep your finger on the pulse early on.

Retreating

> **Jaycee, 35 /** I once saw a movie of a woman being chased and she got inside her door and slammed it shut and then stood there pressed against the door arms outstretched and panting hard that she had escaped her attacker. I felt that way after a few dates and realized that if I was feeling that I couldn't wait to get home and escape, maybe it was not time to be dating.

> **Ken, 42 /** I was out of my relationship for a short period of time and was serial dating. I was just bored and, it sounds rough, but I didn't care about dating or any of the women I was with. I just did it for something to do. When I realized that, I went into full-bore retreat mode.

Getting back out there and testing the waters but realizing you're not yet ready is not the same as retreating. Retreating is more akin to giving up. It's okay to give up for a while to figure out things. It's okay to retreat for a while to discover more about how to navigate the world as a single person. Many times getting back out there requires baby steps, more self-discovery, and learning to be social again without pressuring yourself to date. A client said to me, "Yes, but it's been almost two years. I feel as if I'm hiding out." Clearly she had retreated and *was* hiding out. She had become a workaholic and hadn't retreated just from dating but from everyone and everything. She had three jobs, two of which she didn't need, and she had the convenient "I have to work" excuse to avoid just about everything.

Another woman kept wearing her wedding ring, not because she still cared for her ex-husband but because she didn't want men approaching her. This went on for about six months. When I suggested taking off the ring a couple of days a week to see what happened, she looked at me as if I had told her to kill puppies. We scaled it back to one day a week so she would be comfortable. In retreat mode, you need to decide if you want to stay there or if you want to work on moving out of it slowly. Don't let fear dictate which way you need to go. Make a conscious decision that your retreat is permanent or temporary or accept you are simply unsure of it.

Retreat is about going back and licking your wounds. Most times it's normal and necessary. When you first retreat, you may not be able to figure out if it's normal or pathological. Labels are not important, but you need to put the focus back on you and try to figure out if it's fear or something else. One woman said, "I thought I was afraid of dating, but I realized I was just afraid of online dating or going to clubs. I wanted to meet someone when I was out somewhere living my life, and I did." She went to a concert with some friends and the man behind her kept kicking her seat by accident and apologizing. After a while, they started to joke about it and decided to switch seats. By the end of the evening, they were talking and exchanging numbers. "I wasn't really retreating altogether. I was just retreating from the forms of dating I was doing, preferring it to just happen, as it eventually did."

Others have the opposite opinion, as they want to browse photos and profiles. Still others are in true, full-on retreat and don't want to be bothered with dating right now. That is fine. If you're not ready, that is fine so long as you keep checking in with yourself to figure out how and why you are in retreat. It is important to know which one it is and what you are gaining from being in retreat.

Remember, the Five Rs Are Normal

Don't be scared to find yourself in one of the five Rs. Treat it as a developmental phase between your last breakup and a future relationship. Remember to look at any experience you have as a learning experience and be sure to take away the lessons you need to learn. Be gentle with yourself and remember to affirm, each day, that you are okay and will be okay no matter what.

chapter 6

Becoming Sexual and Becoming Exclusive

Laurence, 42 / I struggle with asking a woman about
her sexual history, but I don't like to take chances
on giving or getting a disease. It's a tough subject to
broach, but one time a woman told me after a condom
broke that she wasn't on birth control. It freaked me out
and since then I've managed to find the courage to ask.

Fran, 46 / I don't have sex with anyone outside a
committed relationship because I have found that to be
too much for my fragile psyche. If I sleep with a man, I
don't want to think he's dating or seeing anyone else.
I don't want to be part of a harem.

Janine, 31 / I wanted to become sexually active but had no idea what I liked anymore. I didn't want to figure it out by bedding multiple partners, but I spent so much time responding to my past lovers, I had no clue what I liked or didn't.

Joan, 40 / I'm between the generation who saved themselves for a relationship and the one that just hooks up with anyone and I'm totally confused.

Many will tell you that becoming sexual and becoming exclusive are the same thing. However, that is certainly not true for everyone. It can differ, depending on where people are in their process, what they want from life, and what sex means to them. It's a generalization to say that sex means less, as far as being a committed gesture, to men than to women, though to some extent it's true. It's not true for everyone, as many times the genders switch. Many women are trying to feel "empowered" by having sex whenever they want it and "friends with benefits" relationships, whereas men have decided that they only want to have sex in a committed, monogamous relationship.

When you try to translate this generalization to same-sex relationships, the waters become even murkier. There are generalizations that gay men have difficulty with monogamy and that lesbians can become enmeshed and jealous. Some say that not only are the generalizations about men and women true, but to prove it, they point to the fact that they become magnified when applied to same-sex relationships.

It becomes less clear for older people who are coming out of long-term marriages and for people who have only had sex in committed relationships and have never experimented or had one-night stands. There are many who have never sown any wild oats, and others who have been crazy enough for everyone. Still, the new landscape is confusing. Older people don't always know the rules, and they are afraid to venture out and more afraid to stay in their cocoons. After all, who is out there now? Only people who have been continually rejected or have continually rejected? Are there other people coming out of long-term relationships who don't know what to do either? Are there many post-fifties walking around wanting a partner but unsure how to find one? Many post-fifties were part of the "sex, drugs, and rock 'n' roll" era but they realize that the sexual landscape has changed as much or even more than they have over the years. Those who were into drugs, sex, and rock 'n' roll may still be into rock 'n' roll, but they consider drugs something they did in their youth and are not so sure about sex since the appearance of HIV, HPV, genital herpes, and hepatitis C.

One woman moped about how things had changed since she was single, over a decade ago: "There's body hair to worry about, sexting, selfies, and assuming a lot of intimacy that doesn't really exist. Some days I just want to crawl under the covers alone and stay there." But younger clients have complaints as well. A twenty-something client lamented, "I date but no one wants to pull the trigger on an exclusive relationship so I don't have the luxury of putting up a lot of rules and regulations. I feel lucky when someone wants to be with me, so I'll pretty much do what he wants." For someone so young, that is a wrong attitude.

The Sexual Inventory

Once you strengthen your self-esteem to become a person of dignity who has choices, you do get to discuss "rules and regulations" as an equal partner in an equal relationship. However, you need to know, before another person even enters the picture, who you are in the sexual sense. In any relationship the goal is to have your partner love and cherish your authentic self. Knowing your authentic sexual self can be a dicey subject and one that can be in flux due to so many variables. If it's that hard to figure out, how do you get to know yourself and then try to present that sexual self to another? The answer is the sexual inventory.

The sexual inventory is similar to the life inventory in that you look at past relationships, your behavior, and needed adjustments to that behavior. Like the life inventory, it may go back to childhood and influences or experiences you had long before your sexual identity was formed. As in the life inventory, it is important to question choices you've made and behaviors you've engaged in simply to be liked or accepted. When you wrote your life inventory, you may or may not have included those who harmed you sexually. Similarly, when you made your list of standards and compatibility, you may not have included sexual behaviors or requests from a partner. In deciding whether or not to be exclusive with a partner, you may need to know if you have sexual compatibility. Before you can enter into the discussion with another person, you must first know what is negotiable, nonnegotiable, and may or may not be negotiable with this person. In defining your sexual self, you must also gauge its relationship to your idea of intimacy. These tasks become easier when broken down carefully. Once you come to know who you are in a sexual sense, you will know if sex and exclusivity is a must or a maybe for you. When you know and accept who you are and what you are, you can convey that to another.

Recall an example I offered about accepting or rejecting a person who looks at pornography. This very well may be a standard that you've developed and not something you consider to be part of your sexual self. One woman said, "I see nothing sexual about pornography so I don't think my dislike of it has anything to do with my sexual self. It's outside my realm, and I want it to be outside the realm of my partner." Another woman said, "I don't like hard-core porn, but I do consider soft porn to be acceptable, enjoyable, and part of who I am sexually." Each woman was comfortable with her particular view and had no reservations about conveying it to a new partner. That is the goal of the sexual inventory. It's about what you are comfortable with and what you can or cannot convey to a partner. It's not about judging or being judged, but simply what issues you may need to address based on past relationships, what questions you need to ask and answer to define who you are sexually at this point in time, and what is negotiable and nonnegotiable and what may be negotiable.

Childhood Trauma and Abuse

There are many people who had no significant negative experiences around sex as a child. Some experienced negativity but outgrew their uneasiness. Still others had experiences that left them scarred, seemingly for good. The need for delving into childhood and adolescent experiences that may have warped the adult sexual experience differs from person to person. No matter what your recollection, it's a good idea to give some thought to your earliest sexual experiences.

1. As you did with the life inventory, make two columns, one for positive and one for negative. Think about your most recent relationship and the sexual traits and proclivities of your partner and put them into the appropriate column. For each trait or proclivity, think about past partners who had similar traits.

2. For your last partner, write about any sexual act you performed that made you uncomfortable. Think back on other partners and list all such experiences.

3. Have you ever felt you had a different level of sexual energy than your partner? How did you feel about it? Are you now looking for someone who shares that or who simply understands yours?

4. Think about your recent relationship and write about your sexual behaviors and tendencies. Which ones are positive and which are negative? Think

back on your sexual partners and write down other relationships where your behaviors were the same.

5. Think back to any sexual experiences you had before you were sexually ready. Were you abused, harassed, teased, or bullied?

6. As an adolescent, did you develop early or late? How did this affect your self-image and self-esteem?

7. Have you been able to openly discuss sex with peers or partners? If not, why not? Have you wondered if you were "normal"? Have you been comfortable with your sexuality?

As with your life inventory, the lists and questions allow you to reference and cross-reference the relationships in your life and see if you are "other oriented" sexually, meaning you are responding to what you think someone else wants rather than knowing what you want.

How Early Experiences Cloud Adult Experiences

There may be sexual abuse, harassment, bullying, or taunting that affected your sexual development. Some of your experiences may require counseling and some may require an exercise to finish business. Review your inventory and identify those that still sting or influence your thinking or behavior. Whether it's overt sexual abuse or the endless taunting of the sixth-grade bully, there are people and situations that are not far from memory when you think back on it.

For each situation, write a letter to the offending party, as you did in your life inventory, and say how you were harmed by what was done and how it has damaged your life. Write that you are working toward letting it go (either in counseling for sexual abuse or by developing affirmations to counter the stinging barbs you can still feel) and that you refuse to allow this person to have anymore power over you. While it may be difficult to forgive, write that you release this person and the harm caused. Spend some time, as you did before, sitting with your thoughts and feelings. When you are ready, read your letter to a counselor or a friend or aloud to yourself, rip it up, and let it go. When it is in shreds, burn it or throw it away with the proclamation, "You have no power over me any longer. I am free to find my authentic sexual self."

The Sexual Standards and Compatibility List

The first standards and compatibilities list was to narrow your choices. It's important to concentrate on defining that list before you embark on a sexual relationship. Practicing your new observation skills and honoring your list is an important component of healthy dating. The next list is the sexual standards and compatibilities list. This list assumes that you are moving toward the place where you are ready to engage in deeper, possibly committed relationships. Now that you are accepting yourself fully, it's time to focus on your sexual list of *negotiable*, *nonnegotiable*, and *maybe negotiable*.

Discovering your authentic sexual self requires reviewing your sexual inventory and your list of sexual standards and compatibilities. If you found that your sexual behaviors and choice of partners are based in trying to fill empty places, wanting to be liked, or being confused, it is time to discover who you are and to embrace it, perhaps for the first time ever. The important thing in developing your authentic sexual self is knowing that you are okay no matter what and if your new partner isn't compatible with you, that doesn't mean it's your fault or you have to change anything. Again, if you decide to change something about yourself, it has to be an informed decision based on the level of compatibility in other areas and the honest desire to give up a little for the right person.

When going through your sexual inventory, note anything that you engaged in because someone else wanted you to do it or because you thought you needed to do it to keep a relationship alive. Many times chaotic relationships will be filled with "toe-curling sex" that is more performance than passion. More than one client has told me that it was difficult to leave a bad relationship when "the sex was so good." Getting swept up in the high wire act that can come from wild makeup sex after a knock-down, drag-out fight causes a person to lose perspective on what truly feels good. Without the wild makeup sex, these couples cannot survive. There is nothing else to connect them. It's time to leave the wild makeup sex in the bedroom and realize that intimacy happens everywhere (not the sex act, but intimacy). Healthy couples do not engage in breakup/makeup cycles. Further, once you relieve yourself of having to be "on" in the bedroom, you can spend some time thinking about what you really like and are willing to do.

One woman said there were certain boundaries that she allowed men to cross that she was not willing to do anymore. "When I looked at my sexual inventory, a feeling of ickiness came over me. There were things I decided to never do again and if that was not okay with my man then he was not the man for me." When I brought up the topic at a women's retreat, most in the room nodded their head. Being real instead of putting on a show is a very difficult change to make, but if you're bringing the real you to a relationship, it has to include an authentic sexual self.

For some people certain questions don't even come up until they are with a new partner who is proposing something they have never done before. One woman said, "My boyfriend kept bringing up his past where he enjoyed bondage, and I stayed silent on the matter. When he pressed it a bit more, I said I was not interested. We didn't last long after that conversation. I was starting to fall in love with him, but I could not handle being tied up or doing it to someone. I had hoped it wasn't a deal breaker, but it was. I wish he had told me sooner." Several people reported similar experiences where sexual preferences kept them apart, but it's not always that way.

One man said, "I like women who talk in bed and have a bit of a wild side, but my girlfriend is never going to be like that. I love everything about her, so her lack of sexual adventure or curiosity isn't going to send me packing or seeking out others." Differing sexual preferences may indicate whether a relationship is going the distance and sometimes it does not. While it's a difficult subject to bring up, it's worth knowing. As always, know what you want and what is negotiable and nonnegotiable. For the man who wanted bondage, it was nonnegotiable, yet the man who wanted wild sex and had a conservative girlfriend was willing to forgo the wildness.

So whether gay or straight, young or old, having a lot of experience with a lot of people or only having some with a few, it's difficult to go into dating situations with preconceived notions about physical contact. A woman coming out of a long-term marriage wanted to broach it with her guy, who seemed to be very sensual and interested in going further and had not been in a committed relationship in a long time. He hinted at many short-term relationships. After thinking about it and practicing her speech for days, she mustered up the courage to say, "I was married a long time. I don't know what people do these days about deciding to have sex, but I'm uncomfortable about it if a person hasn't been tested." He offered to get the testing done so she would feel more at ease, but when she asked how many one-night stands he had in his life, he said, "Let's just say probably more than you have had and less than you think I've had."

That was the perfect answer. Telling someone exactly how many partners you've had, especially if the number is high, is not reassuring. It's not something a new person wants to imagine and probably not something you want to think about. You have to balance enough information and too much. You do not want to hear all the details or numbers nor do you want to tell all, whether you are a man or woman, young or old, gay or straight. Every person should be cautious, and asking someone to take an HIV or STD test is not out of line. Many insist on using condoms and then if a long-term relationship is on the horizon, talk about STD testing before forgoing the use of condoms. No matter who you are or what you have or have not done, safe sex is an absolute necessity at the beginning of a relationship.

There may be times when you are "sexually unsure," meaning you are not clear what your standards are. You may experiment with casual sex or, if coming out of a long-term relationship, want to know what it's like to be with someone else. You may feel vulnerable and wind up in situations that you feel are not truly who you are. One woman said, "I never think about some of the men I've been with. It's hard when you're halfway through a sexual encounter and realize you just want out. It's not their sexual prowess, but just a realization that this is the wrong guy, the wrong time, the wrong everything. Sometimes they will come into my conscience and I will wonder 'what was I thinking?' and I wish I had a huge eraser for the whole night. Thankfully I've never gotten an STD or pregnant as I've insisted on safe sex, but there's been too many of those nights and it's not who I am; it's a phase I went through a few times after a breakup."

Distancing yourself from distasteful sexual memories is not a bad thing. Guilt is a useless emotion except when it leads you to make amends to someone still in your life. Get rid of all guilt you've had about sexual activity you've engaged in but are not proud of. This goes for everyone. One man confessed that he felt guilty toward some insensitive things he did to early girlfriends and women who were one-night stands. As he matured, the relationships started to bother him, and he went far out of his way to please the women he was with to his own detriment.

"I absolutely lost sight of what I liked and who I liked and what I wanted to be doing. It was about pleasing a woman as some kind of crazy punishment for how I was in my twenties."

If you are on the path to finding real love, it's time to clarify your sexual standards as to who, when, where, and how. No matter who you are, sexual activity is going to cloud your perspective on your choice of partners. One interviewee said, "I was seeing a nice guy and moving along slowly. An ex-boyfriend came to town and I spent the night with him. I was so guilty that I started to pull away from the new guy. I had committed to 'no sex outside of a committed relationship' as a standard and was on the road to a committed relationship. I had been celibate and was sure that we were going to have sex soon, but a drunken reunion got in the way. It was terrible." Feeling guilty, she pulled away for a while, explaining to the man she had "a lot going on" and needed to take a break from dating. She worked through her guilt, returned to him, and picked up where they left off and developed a beautiful relationship. She never told him about the one-night stand with the ex and that was for the best, as they were not committed to each other at the time and she didn't want to hurt him. She worked through her guilt and the issues left over from the ex-boyfriend before returning to him. I concurred with her decision that some things do not need to be shared, only learned from. This was one of those things.

Another woman said, "The guy was giving me mixed signals. We were very close friends for a few months but there was a definite physical attraction. After a long day spent holding hands and being playful, we started kissing. I pushed the envelope to go back to his place. We made love and it was just okay. In the morning, he was confused and upset that it happened so soon. He wanted to determine the rhythm, and we agreed to stop seeing each other, even as friends. I was heartbroken and felt horrible about myself." Despite her displeasure and his unwillingness to see her again, they met up several times over the course of the next year and the same thing happened each time. The last time they were together, he asked her to sleep over. In the morning he told her how much he loved her and was grateful for her. She left thinking they were finally back on the road to a relationship, but she never heard from him again. She says, "I still don't know if we were just friends with benefits or if we had a shot at a relationship. We were very close and loved each other but when I took him off his pace, I wrecked what could have been a good thing." Although many a guy will push for sex, some will not and don't appreciate it if a woman does before he's ready.

Hindsight is 20/20 and they obviously had a "thing," just not the thing she wanted it to be. Looking back, she would have asked what was going on but even that might have scared him away if he wasn't ready or didn't know. Despite that gut-wrenching experience, she again pushed a man into a sexual relationship before he was ready. In therapy she figured out that "leaving her stamp" on a guy was her endgame. She wanted to be unforgettable but was making it happen in the worst way possible.

After she discovered this flaw in the system, she stopped leaving her mark on a man and concentrated on building healthy relationships. She insisted on having "the talk"—where things were going and how they were going to get there. It was hard and uncomfortable at first, but—again—this should be an in-person talk. She said that as soon as a guy gave her a "deer in the headlights" look, she knew he had no intention investing in a long-term relationship. Quickly moving away from those types, she started to find men who were looking for the long-term and happy to talk about it before bedding down. "My friends all say that you have to have sex with someone *before* you talk about a relationship because suppose they're not very good in bed? I don't think the guy that I was crazy about and slept with too soon was a great lover, but I would have settled for mediocre sex and a great relationship. Instead, I pushed him into sex, found it mediocre, and blew the chance at a relationship. Many of my friends want sex to be off the charts and that's their prerogative, but for me I want someone who cares and is okay in bed at the very least."

One thing that needs to be on your list of standards is how high sex ranks in importance. Depending on your age and circumstances, it may not be as high as another person's. One man said, "My friends talk about sex all the time when once or twice a week would be fine with me. I hesitate to tell women this as I don't want them to think there's something wrong with me, but I really don't want to be with a woman who is not happy with the infrequency of sex." When a man approaches a woman with the idea that he's not looking for sex as frequently as most women think most men are, both may hesitate. It's an odd conversation and neither is comfortable. Again, it may be negotiable or nonnegotiable. There are both men and women who have a lower than average libido but may find that no one has yet lit that fire. In the beginning, it's good to talk some, act some, and see where you are compatible or may need to compromise. You may think the quality of sex is negotiable and then go out with someone who is a bad lover. Where sexual compatibility is concerned, you can have levels of negotiability. For example, if a person is a great lover but bad partner, the partner part is nonnegotiable. If a person is a mediocre lover but good partner, the sex part is negotiable. If a person is a bad lover but a good partner, you have to make a decision depending on how bad a lover and how good a partner.

A woman who had been with a string of high-octane lovers said she fell in love with a guy who planned a night each week where they soaked in his Jacuzzi tub with candles lit in the bathroom, fresh flowers in the bedroom and bath, and rose petals all over the floor in both rooms. They had long hours of foreplay and much cuddling afterward. "We sometimes had morning sex on another day or two, but I'd rather have one night of what he gave than seven nights of fifteen-minute sex. But if he had told me he only liked sex once a week, I would have bolted. I'm glad I experienced what that one night was like before we talked about it."

The Timing of Sexual Intimacy

You may be in a place, right after a relationship ends, where you do want to be with someone else as soon as possible. A woman who was in a loveless marriage for a long time began dating the night her husband moved out. She didn't sleep with the first couple of guys but soon started on the second and third date as well as becoming "flirty" with a very married man on her job. She was sure the flirtation was mutual, but if it wasn't, it was a huge gamble on her part; when he started to suspect her interest, he distanced himself from it as a married man should. Fleeing a loveless, perhaps sexless marriage after debating about it for so long had clouded her perspective to the point where she almost allowed it to infect her work environment. She had joined two online dating sites and had been with over a dozen guys in the first few months.

Sex on a first date is something I advise against for anyone who is seeking a forever love. People who are newly dating should take things slow so they can assess the other's potential to be a suitable partner. Sex can cloud the issue of compatibility. You may be sizzling red-hot lovers, but you may not be compatible in other areas. The earlier you have sex, the less likely you are to see the other person objectively. A male client of mine says sex by the fourth date is imperative. His motto is, "Bed or dead." I have some female clients who would disagree and ask for more time to assess things. However, a female client of mine had been on seven dates with a man she described as "nice and attentive." By that time he had not even kissed her. He told her he had very close relationships with his sisters and almost all his close friends were women. I told her, "Okay, you don't need a best friend. You want a boyfriend. Drop him." There are too early and too late scenarios and you have to decide for yourself, on your sexual inventory and by reviewing your sexual history, which one it is.

Another client said, "We had powerful chemistry and our first few dates were hours long. We laughed and talked so much and he kept saying how adorable I was. He was newly divorced and getting used to the dating scene, and I pushed the sex thing a bit too soon. He wasn't ready and I had never met a man who wasn't ready, so I just powered ahead. We ended shortly thereafter and I never again initiated sex with a guy. I put that on my sexual inventory and I never deviated from it, with good results."

When you first break up, you may go a bit wild for a while, but when you get serious about being in relationship mode, frivolous sexual activity should stop, whether a casual night with an ex or an ongoing "friends with benefits" situation you've been in to ease the pain. If you have been sexually active, you want to get yourself tested before you begin dating and then retested in six months if you've been very sexually active and now want to find a serious relationship. The idea of "keeping your side of the street clean" includes being conscientious about your health, sexual and otherwise.

Most couples attend to their sexual compatibility early in the relationship. Others take what they get. Some are very concerned about staying with someone for the long term who is not sexually compatible. Again, this is a "depends who you are" issue. There are some who can and will rethink what they need sexually if a person is terrific in every other way. Others will insist that sexual compatibility comes first and if it's not there, the relationship—no matter how great a person is—is going nowhere.

If they are not compatible and they continue dating, each must take responsibility for that. There is no sense in being involved with someone who is not on the same sexual page as you unless you concretely decide that it's okay. It can be something as simple as one partner wants a light on, one wants it dark, and they compromise by lighting a candle. However, frequency and openness can be issues. Sometimes a couple has boiling chemistry when they are dating, but after they are together awhile, one changes it to barely a simmer. That can lead to teary accusations, mistrust, occasional threats of leaving the relationship, or suspicions of infidelity. One may be thinking "you no longer find me desirable," whereas the lowered libido is purely physical and not emotional. It may not reflect how much or how little they want their partner. It happens as people get older or experience physical issues or sometimes for no apparent reason, but it's not always a reflection of the love toward their partner.

Seeing a doctor can help, and there are medications available for both men and women. Understanding it's a physical thing and not an emotional thing is important. If it is an emotional thing, it is very difficult for most couples to see a sex therapist, but they can sit down in unity and talk about what they each need and come to an understanding around it. As the woman whose mate wanted to have sex only one night a week but made it a truly memorable experience with the Jacuzzi and the rose petals, she found ground she didn't know existed. Another man had a similar experience as his wife proposed a date night that included dinner, a movie, a hot tub, and sex to top off the evening. Though he wanted greater frequency, he said that they held hands in the movie, which they hadn't done since they were dating, and he felt closer to her on date night than he had in a long time. At first he resisted the idea, thinking he was giving up a lot, but the idea of making it an event night actually worked out well for them. During the week, he didn't press and she didn't decline, which previously had caused them both to go sulking to separate corners. Another woman said she didn't like oral sex but they gave and received on their birthdays and anniversary. "I'm sure he'd like it much more and I'd like it never, but that's what we've agreed on and it works."

It may be a matter of finding where you both can reside and feel good about it. The solution for a happy sex life is not a matter of liking the same frequency, same amount of foreplay, or the same positions, but the perception that you have a sex life that is satisfying for both of you. In all these examples, the resolution was a compromise that took each into consideration. Because of romantic love songs and movies, couples expect searing, curl-your-toes sex every time. But in the wake of babies, jobs, and other responsibilities, that level of sexual activity can fall by the wayside quickly. The solution is to find the middle ground, respond to each other's concerns and desires, and address them as evenhandedly as you can.

The Complications of Sexual Activity

On your sexual inventory list, it's important to remind yourself of the pitfalls of unprotected sex, casual sex, and the like. Lying in the arms of a lover can feel good but can also leave you facing a situation you really don't want. Keep these items in mind:

Pregnancy

The number of never married mothers is at an all-time high. This is not an issue if a woman has good financial resources, a drama-free life, a great support system, and has made a decision to have a child with a man that she knows well and will be a decent father to her child. The problem starts when a woman is not financially stable, fails to take birth control seriously, becomes pregnant, and then breaks up with the father. The ensuing years can be a nightmare for all, especially the child.

There is no reason to have a child with a person you do not know. Whether you are a man or a woman, take proper birth control precautions before you have sex. So many people say they were using birth control and it "failed." In 2014 that's a fairly preposterous notion if you're over a certain age. An accidental pregnancy should be outdated, although it seems common and to an extent socially acceptable. Acceptance of single parenthood is okay, but being chained to someone you hate and makes your child miserable is not. Don't play with Russian roulette with something as important as pregnancy. Use birth control.

Even the most committed partners should think about the ramifications of an unplanned pregnancy. Not only will there be great expense, but the presence of a baby may well strain a relationship beyond its limits. Most who become first-time parents, even those who cared for their younger siblings early on, find the task to be challenging emotionally, mentally, physically, and financially. It should be a well thought out decision of a loving couple and not a reckless act with the potential to tether you to someone you are not going to be able to deal well with for eighteen long years.

Catching a disease is one thing, but having an unplanned child with someone who could turn out to be emotionally damaged, uncooperative, abusive, or morally deficient enough to hide money to avoid paying support is quite another thing. It's not just that it's stupid, but it's unfair to bring an innocent child into this situation. Wait until you have birth control secured or assured before you put yourself in a position to become an "accidental" parent.

STDs

You can contract countless diseases from unprotected sex. I am always surprised at men and women who regularly engage in unprotected sex. One client told me, "I assume that someone is disease free." Why would anyone assume that? I also have clients with STDs who "forget" to tell a potential partner or hide it. Not every person who claims to have been recently tested has been. One woman said she told her soon-to-be-boyfriend about a reoccurring problem of genital warts. She thought they were contained but then they would flare up again. His chances of developing them were not high, but he was at risk for carrying the HPV virus that is also known to generate genital warts. It may not have had a thing to do with it, but before they had a chance to see each other again, he broke up with her.

He didn't know anything about genital warts, but it doesn't sound like something you want to find out about someone *after* you've slept together. If you have sex with someone you really like before saying you have an STD, how do you bring it up without looking bad? It is usually better to be in a place where you've spent time talking, getting to know each other, and you're both smitten before having the "sex talk," revealing STDs and then having sex. It's natural to feel awkward and nervous when disclosing an STD to a partner. Beforehand, practice how you are going to tell your partner, be very specific about it, and ask your partner if there are any questions or time to process it. Give your partner as much clinical information as you can. It's difficult to be up front about an STD, but imparting clinical information with personal experience will help a new partner make a well-informed decision. One woman found a person had not called her because her nervous and awkward revelation scared him.

Not everyone will be scared off so long as you have been treated, and you know how to handle an outbreak and what you can do to prevent your partner from getting infected. Before the STD talk, one woman joked with her soon-to-be-lover, "Guess what my ex-boyfriend gave me?" Not everyone can be humorous about it, but she read her new partner correctly; he was okay and teased her for a long time about how she let him know. Others will be fine with a more serious conversation, but try to gauge how you will present it in light of your partner's personality and style. Again, be as informative and honest as you can be.

Let's say you discover you have an STD while you're in a relationship. It may come from your partner or from a former lover. Some STDs do not show up for some time, so don't immediately accuse your partner of cheating on you. It's a serious matter and you both need to be tested and treated. If your partner did not contract the STD, twice yearly testing is a good idea. An STD does not need to end a relationship and if a couple can work with it and around it, they have a good chance of success in other areas that may be difficult to navigate.

Sexting

Ten years ago, no one knew what a selfie was. Today some people send photos of their most intimate body parts to others they don't even know. It's perfectly fine to text photos of yourself that are amusing, funny, cute, or flirty. But photos of your private parts can turn up all over the Internet. One woman said an ex-boyfriend sent her nude selfie to every person in her life, including her parents. That's extreme, but a person who is angry will use any weapon at hand, and sometimes it's a weapon you've handed them. Try not to send photos that you wouldn't show the world at large. A bad breakup may result in those photos becoming a means of vengeance.

Sexual texting exchanges may sound like good old-fashioned phone sex except for the fact that texting is on the record and, again, can be used against you. If you really don't care if one day your texts turn up everywhere, go ahead. However, if you're unsure or don't really want to do it, don't. Long-distance sex typically involves fantasy, and if your fantasies are things you would never consider in real life, that will not be apparent when your ex shows those texts to the world.

Another pitfall is that if you send a sexually explicit text or photo to someone who is not ready for it, it can be considered sexual harassment. Talk about it first. Careless politicians have taught us that sexting and selfies can be ways to cheat without actually cheating. It's fulfilling a sexual fantasy that a married person is having with you. Your personal morals, values, boundaries, and limits come into play with that. Figure out how much or how little you want to participate before you meet a cute person at a conference who lives three thousand miles away and convinces you that sexting is fun and flirty.

The positive side of sexting is that it can be a fun way to let someone know what you like in bed. For many, sexting it is easier than talking in person. You can sext about fantasies if you like, but only ones that you might actually consider. Be careful not to blur the line between "what I'd like and am willing to do" with "this is just a sexual fantasy I would never play out in real life." It can be a great way to let your new lover know what you like and how you like it, and ask if anything is missing for your partner. If your partner states a preference for something out of the question, you can text back, "I'm not into something like that. Is it a deal breaker?" Or you can think about it. A woman said her boyfriend asked her about anal sex via text and she shot back, "Absolutely not." He responded, "I thought so. No problem!" When they talked about it, he said he was curious but it was fine, as he was getting along without it anyway.

Their mixture of texting and face-to-face communication was great. He broached a very sensitive subject via text and they followed up with real conversation. But don't allow your texting relationship to replace your real-world relationship because that is where trouble happens. If you've sexted or had serious communication via text, it's difficult to stop it. Before you get into anything like that, lay the ground rules that there will be no sexting and no serious communication, especially regarding sex and exclusivity, over text or email. It's imperative that texting not get out of hand and not be used as a tool to communicate important matters. While it can be used to broach sensitive subjects, most important matters should be discussed over the phone or in person. Don't allow texting to become your main form of communication.

Bringing Up Being Divorced

You dated, mated, married, and divorced or an equivalent where you were in a long-term relationship. Sometimes you meet someone wonderful before your divorce is final because your ex is being stubborn about legal things. Keep conversation about recently ended relationships very light in the beginning of a new relationship. When the relationship starts to become exclusive, you can shed a bit more light on the subject or ask your partner to, but avoid gory details. If you and your ex have an antagonistic relationship, do not make your new partner the target of your anger. This new person is not a sounding board about sensitive subjects—problems with the ex being the most popular one. If you have friends, a mother, a therapist, or other people close to you, talk to them about your ex and your ongoing issues.

One woman said, "I told my new, never married boyfriend so much of what kind of games my ex was playing and how much it upset me. He asked his mother for advice as to how to comfort me, but instead of advice, she suggested that he not stay involved with me. The first time I met her, she was cool and standoffish. When I told my boyfriend how uncomfortable I was, he told me she thought I was full of drama and would be for a long time to come. Weeks later he broke up with me because he thought his mother had good instincts and saw my drama with my ex, even though it was completely manufactured by my ex, as a huge red flag." Crushed by the ending, she blamed him for not saying something sooner. Many won't say anything to you as you rant and rave about your ex, but you don't know what they are thinking.

If your new person has gone through a terrible divorce or has a cantankerous ex who causes problems around visitation or support, you can be supportive, but try not to get deeply involved. If it's seriously affecting your relationship, you may need to think about what it means for the long term. In any case, try to take a hands-off approach. Your new partner's ex is not going to be happy when the new love suddenly has opinions about their divorce, separation, or children. You butting in can make thing worse for everyone.

Becoming Exclusive

The idea of asking someone for exclusivity terrifies most people. Many women do not want to seem needy or pushy; many men don't want to appear jealous or controlling, and some just don't know how to word it. Shedding your clothes and having sex seems easier than asking about commitment. Some know that exclusivity is expected of them but they have some attachment/commitment issues and "go along to get along." So although there are many signs that you are indeed exclusive, you should find out how committed you each are by way of conversation. Like sexual subjects, this might be another time where texting has a place. It is easier to ask questions over text, but follow up with real conversation.

Nonverbal signs of exclusivity include being introduced to friends, going to important social occasions together, meeting each other's families, and having a lot of regular or scheduled time together. A friend said they did not have "the talk" for weeks. Her future boyfriend invited her to a party but, for networking purposes, he needed to mingle and talk shop at certain points without her by his side. Being independent, this was fine with her but as she wandered around the room, other men would come up and talk to her, and suddenly her date would reappear and be obnoxiously possessive. Yet he kept glancing around the room and was not attentive when they were alone. Confused, she texted him the next day, "If we're not on the same page, that's fine, but I really need to know. People ask me if I have a boyfriend and I say yes, but maybe I don't." He was glad she brought it up and said he always considered them exclusive, as he never dated more than one person at a time. She had no idea that was his standard, and it would have saved them both a lot of grief had he said that in the beginning as it was also her standard. The most common way of broaching the subject is asking if your partner is seeing anyone else or mentioning that you have stopped seeing anyone else.

In my own life, my husband broached it a little less delicately. At the end of our third date, which went on hours longer than we thought it would, and after several long nights spent talking on the phone, he said, "Can I tell everyone at work I have a girlfriend?" I laughed and said yes. Another man said something similar when inviting a woman to a family event. Driving there, he said, while keeping his eyes on the road, "I want to let them know that you're the person I'm seeing, and I'm not interested in seeing anyone else. How does that sound to you?" To clarify she asked if he was saying they were exclusive and when he said yes, she agreed to both the way he was presenting her and the idea of being exclusive. Another woman, also driving to a family event, asked the guy if he was seeing others. She wasn't willing to be one of many, and she would introduce him as a friend if she were. He said, "You're the only one I'm interested in and if it's agreeable to you, I'd like it that we're both only seeing only each other." Everyone has a different way to go about it, most find it uncomfortable and tense, but play to your strengths and your partner's. I was astounded at how many interviewees asked the question while driving. You have to keep your eyes on the road and if the answer is no, you don't have to worry about it.

If you are going to ask a question, be prepared for any answer and when bringing up the idea of exclusivity, especially when you have control of a car, make sure that you have a follow-up line or conversation planned if the answer is no. What are you willing to do at this point? You can wait, but how long? You can deliver an ultimatum, but you must be prepared to act on it. You can pull away from the relationship and see if this person misses you. While it may sound like a game, pulling back is a protection for you. You need time to think, feel, and then come to an "accept it, change it, or leave" decision. You can just accept the nonexclusivity and start dating others yourself. The last option is often misery.

What you don't want to do is harangue someone about this. If that person is not ready, find out why and see if you can do anything to help. If they don't want exclusivity ever, you need to know why. Is it just with you or with anyone? Are there concerns that you can address? Is there something about you that needs to change? Are you being assessed properly? Is it that the "certain something" isn't there? Is it that the person has waited for a heart flutter, weak knees experience with you and it hasn't happened yet? Are there red flags that are not red flags for you? Getting more information without harassing someone is important. Be careful to modulate your tone and keep it as civil and open-minded as possible. Gather as much information as you can and take away from it what you are given.

Should Sex and Exclusivity Be Related?

There are many who think that attaching sex to exclusivity is old-fashioned or beside the point. There are others who think that in a perfect world, sex and exclusivity go hand in hand. You and your partner are both falling fast, have no desire to see anyone else, and so it's not even a question that you're exclusive. You know you are because you're both starry-eyed when you're together. You may avoid the term "falling in love," but you know that is what you are doing. Sometimes one person falls fast and the other takes a while to catch up. In any case, it is preferable for the feelings to precede full-blown sexual involvement. It's okay to make that a standard and discuss that standard with your partner. Many will honor and even appreciate it. It keeps people from relationships of convenience, reduces the number of sex partners a person has, and makes a statement as to the importance each person places on both love and making love.

When Exclusivity/Commitment Becomes an Issue

When you first go back out into the dating world, it feels strange and unnatural to "date around" after you've found someone you click with and really like and who likes you. Sometimes one party falls in love first and that can create tension. One person doesn't want to see anyone else while the other is unsure. Ambivalence on the part of one may reflect ambivalence on the part of the other. Sometimes a person seeking a serious relationship keeps picking unavailable people. If that is your situation, look at your life inventory and your sexual inventory and figure out if a fear of intimacy or true connection is at play here and why. Sometimes just understanding that you actually desire real love helps you figure out why you are still getting into short-term relationships with people unable to commit.

There are books, treatises, and endless arguments about emotional unavailability in both men and women. For those who suffer from being unavailable, exclusivity and commitment are an issue. The problem may be temporary (just coming off a breakup or having experienced a major life change) or may be permanent. The trouble is that you don't know and, many times, the person with the issue doesn't either. You play games with each other, try to manipulate the relationship into what you want it to be, and both come out on the losing end.

Relationships fall apart at this stage or the couple plays a come here/go away game until one gets sick of it. It's important to know what you plan to do with someone you truly care for who seems to have commitment issues. It is very unsettling to attempt to unravel the deep mysteries of the emotionally unavailable and, at this stage of the game, you shouldn't have to do that. If someone is not committing, doesn't want to commit, or flees every time the subject comes up, a healthy person will usually choose to leave. If you're hanging in there with someone who has commitment issues, revisit your life inventory to see if this is a pattern and decide if it needs to change.

Someone may be ambivalent or just not ready. If they need more time, you need to figure out how much. If they are brand-new to the dating scene after many years, they may be advised to date around and not commit for a year or so (many people are given crazy advice from well-meaning friends and family with regard to time frames). If you're the very first one to date a person who has had a divorce or major breakup, you may have drawn the short straw. No matter how happy or compatible you seem, a person who isn't ready to be back into a committed relationship will refuse to be. If you have chemistry, there may be some stalling about letting you know this, but eventually it needs to be in the open and you need to be willing to walk and not to wait. Think about it and come up with a guideline for yourself. "If she's not ready in six months, I'm going to end it." For many it's okay to wait six months and for others, it's six weeks. You need to decide for yourself how long you're going to wait and why. You can't have a fruitful discussion with your partner if you don't know where you stand on things. A female client waited almost a year only to find out that he saw her more as a friend and a bridge to "real" girlfriends.

Ultimatums

Ultimatums are given when you need an answer to a question, and you are ready to handle *any* answer. Do not deliver one if you're not ready to act. If you think someone probably needs six months to be committed, discuss it. If they seem unsure, give yourself another month to bring it up again. If they don't know by then, you may need to deliver an ultimatum.

Ultimatums sound scary and painful but they need not be. You can say, "I understand your reluctance to commit, or even to commit to when you can commit, but I have to know by Christmas where we stand; otherwise I'm going to move on." The only time to do this is when you are indeed ready to move on at Christmas. Think ultimatums out carefully and try to keep both of your needs in mind. Most of all, don't deliver an ultimatum that is merely a line in the sand.

When You're Both Ready to Commit

Early relationships often blossom on the wings of chemistry, romance, and the good feeling of being with someone again. When the initial feelings wear off, you may be left with someone you don't like very much. However, you may be left with someone you are compatible with and who will make a great partner, but you're missing the early attachment. All good relationships come down to earth and live in the real world. Infatuation does not allow a real-world relationship to exist. It takes two people who have a strong sense of self, interests beyond the relationship, support beyond the relationship, and enough compatibility to find both love and friendship in a committed relationship.

If your relationship cannot survive beyond the early stages, don't be hard on yourself. Many revert to, "I'll never find anyone," or other modes of negative thinking. Remember your affirmations and self-care. After your initial disappointment fades, get back to positive thinking and try to be glad you had this experience with this person, take from it what you need to learn, and move on, perhaps unhappily but definitely healthier. Don't settle for less than you deserve and don't abandon your list: Someone who wants to be with me. If that is your standard, you will find it.

chapter 7

The Ex and the Children: Timing Is Everything

Michael, 47 / I have to admit that I introduced all my love interests to my children way too soon. One of the issues was timing. If we didn't do that, we'd never see each other. Now I know it's worth the scheduling difficulties to wait.

Gina, 34 / I kept scheduling play dates for my kids when I had dates. I realized I was pushing them to the back of my life and they were sensing it was for a guy. I had to stop and spend time with them so they didn't feel left out or replaced.

Jerry, 44 / Every time my ex learns I'm seeing someone, the problems start. There's not enough child support, I don't go to enough games, I'm not involved enough. I don't know how to balance my ex and her needs and the need to become involved with someone and spend some of my rare free time with her.

No subject is more sensitive than your children and the new person in your life or your new person's children. This is complicated by the relationships you have with the children's other parent and your new person has with their co-parent. It becomes even more complicated when the other parents also have new partners.

To be fair to your children, you may start and stop several relationships before you get to one serious enough to introduce your children to your new partner. The last thing children need is a parade of people who are parents, stepparents, semistepparents, Mom's or Dad's partner or date or friend. The idea is not to keep the line moving but to avoid a line at all until there is someone very special.

Therefore, I strongly suggest that you don't introduce children to dates who are not serious relationships. Even if your incredibly inquisitive nine-year-old daughter asks you directly if you're dating anyone, you can say yes you are but it's nothing serious. Sometimes, children fear that you will attend to your new love and not them, so it is imperative you finish the discussion with the fact that she is your child and you will love her and be there for her no matter what. Children are not adept at expressing feelings sometimes, especially when they feel insecure. They may not even acknowledge the insecurity, but it's a good idea to assure them all the same whenever dating or relationships come into play.

When it is time to share a relationship, keep the information very broad and omit the details. You are not obligated to share your love life with your children or let them in on whether or not you are actively dating. Even after you have become exclusive and are working toward a committed relationship, what you are doing, and how you are doing it, should not become a family matter until it's going to be a family matter.

Children need time to adjust to any new person in their life, so until you have absolutely decided that this relationship is going to be serious and long-term, it is not a good idea to introduce your children to your partner. In the meantime, you and your partner can use this time to see how you both interact with the other parent of your children. Not every relationship has to be, or can be, amicable, but not every ex is the evil parent and not every person you pick is the good and righteous parent just trying to do what is best for the children. It is important to note the dynamics between the parents.

Exes, Kids, Stepkids: Who Fits Where?

Many a budding relationship starts to sink as soon as the ex-spouse learns of a new person's existence. For many of my clients, things worsen as soon as an ex suspects that a new person is in the picture. A client of mine stated that when her new boyfriend's ex found out about her, the requests and the demands placed on him were magnified. His ex-wife suddenly had parties and important things to attend on his weekend off and needed him to watch their children. Before my client began seeing him, none of these events occurred. The ex started to chunk the time he spent with the kids, spreading it over a weekend rather than him having them all weekend or not at all for the weekend, as he had before. Because he felt guilty that his behavior had caused the deterioration of the marriage, he capitulated to all her demands. This made it impossible for them to go away together or to spend uninterrupted weekends together.

Since you cannot change the ex or leave the ex, you must accept the ex, warts and all. What matters is what your new partner does. Many times someone who feels guilty for a breakup will kowtow to demands. If the ex can treat your partner like a puppet on a string, then you have a problem. And if you get upset over this dynamic, you appear to be interfering with your partner and the children. Any partner who can't or won't make changes in this situation is going to buck you on the issue and take the fallback position that it's "for the children." That is something you cannot argue with and you are boxed in. That is important to note because you may find yourself in an untenable position for the long term. Can you live with a partner who refuses to address or defuse the demands of an overbearing ex? You have to decide.

If your partner's ex is using the kids as pawns and your partner refuses to say anything or, worse, see anything, then you have a problem on your hands that you may or may not be able to navigate. Get honest with yourself about your ability to deal with this repeatedly. Do you want to spend your life watching your partner drop everything (including you) and run when the ex calls?

Another woman said her boyfriend, who had custody of his three-year-old daughter, came home from picking her up on Sunday and the little girl gave her a kiss and then started looking under the couch and behind the chairs. When asked what she was looking for, the little girl replied, "The girlfriend. Mommy says I have to stay away from the girlfriend." She thought of her dad's girlfriend simply as "Mary," a nice lady who visited once in a while. They were slowly getting to know each other and Mary did not force herself on the little girl. Their relationship had been flourishing to the point that when dad tried to dress her or comb her hair, the little girl asked for Mary to do it.

It was obvious that the little girl did not associate Mary with the big, bad "girlfriend" that her mother had mentioned, but nonetheless had been frightened by the idea of this mythical creature called a "girlfriend" who was scary, mean, and to be avoided. Neither the father nor his girlfriend said anything and the child soon went about her business not worrying about the mythical monster, but they were careful to start using "GF" instead of the actual word when introducing Mary around. It was plain that the mother had spent the weekend filling the girl's head full of terrible things about "the girlfriend." If your ex or your partner's ex is going to fill a child's head with horror stories about you, there will be a tough row to hoe.

Redirection worked for this couple, but if the child or children are older, it might not. A healthy couple will help older children by allowing the new person to slowly become part of their lives. A jealous ex who makes things tough might be an obstacle in new love, but if you are both committed to a new relationship, it can work. If your ex or your partner's ex makes everyone miserable whenever the kids are around the new person, there may come a time when the ex needs to be spoken to. It's a delicate situation and the new person should have as little as possible to do with it. Blended families can and do work. In the beginning, you want to observe how your partner handles this. If your partner is always going to capitulate to the ex, then you want that information so you can accept it, change it, or leave.

When Do You Introduce a New Partner to Your Children?

It's always hard to place an exact time frame on when to introduce children to a new partner but I usually suggest that parents give younger children, say under the age of eight, at least a year from when you separated and six months for older children.

This may seem like a long time to you, but for them it's not. Too many couples just rush in and see how the children get along. That's not fair to the children nor is it fair to their other parents. One woman reported that her ex wanted their children to blend with his girlfriend's children as soon as possible. They were young (first and second graders), and he wanted them to think of the new kids as siblings. Children of that age may put up a good front, as if they enjoy their new playmates, but many times they are simply doing what Mommy or Daddy wants them to do. When the mother objected to the children meeting so soon (just weeks after separation), the father exploded and accused her of not wanting him to have a nice family. She didn't care if he had ten nice families, she simply cared about the impact on her children, which seemed negative. They came home and complained about the other children and the new girlfriend and wailed that they just wanted Daddy to "come home." Children need time to adapt to the fact that their parents are living apart and are not coming back together before they are introduced to a new love and other children. In this instance, the children may have handled the parental separation a bit better if given time to deal with it before other children and a new love came on the scene. They never got over the early trauma and resented the new wife and her children for years to come. Therefore, it's a good idea to wait before introducing children to a new partner.

However, there is such a thing as waiting too long. I had a boyfriend who introduced me to his teenage kids from his first marriage though he had never introduced them to anyone, including a second wife and daughter, their baby sister. After the first wife found out about me, things escalated to the point where I could not be in his life. Their son went in for surgery and she told him, "No girlfriends are to be at the hospital." I had no plans to go to the hospital, but she was terribly unhappy and in attack mode. I had my own children and did not think it was my place. Instead of explaining this to her, he meekly agreed. He was being punished for taking a stand by introducing them to me and now he was being tormented until he backed down and promised her he would never allow them to be near me.

It works the opposite way as well. If your new partner is insisting on being present whenever you are with your children, then there is an issue. A new person is a virtual stranger to the kids, to the situation, and to the other parent. Give everyone plenty of time to get to know your new partner and don't force this person into the kids' or your ex's life. If your new partner appears to be pushing you in regard to the kids or the ex, gently remind your partner that this might not be the best approach for everyone. A gradual inclusion usually works best for everyone and new partners should understand they are virtual strangers and need to tread lightly.

Red Flags: Observe and Heed the Warnings

Whether you are the new partner or have the new partner, everyone needs to know their place. While your new partner may have been lax in setting boundaries and conditions with the ex, it's not your place to suddenly wage war over visitation, child support, or time spent with the kids. The new partner's ex is going to pick up on the fact that you are the sudden change and that can spell disaster for everyone. You don't know the history, and the one you are hearing might not be telling the truth. Even if you think you're a natural-born problem solver and your new love needs your help, it's important to sit back and use your power of observation before you jump into the fray.

Whether you are the new partner or have the new partner, the new partner needs to know their place is not "full steam ahead" to douse the involvement of the ex.

A client of mine complained that her new boyfriend dropped everything when his ex called. She observed that the ex-wife used the children as pawns by withholding visitation when her boyfriend did not do as she asked. Another client complained that the children were dropped off at random times by her new boyfriend's ex and she would have to leave as soon as they heard her car. It's not just the ex that is the problem. One client observed her boyfriend was thousands of dollars behind in child support and though he said his ex was "bleeding him dry," that is usually not the case. Another client said his new girlfriend rarely saw her children and he wasn't sure if she supported them at all. She too blamed her ex for the sad state of affairs where her children were concerned. Another client observed that his girlfriend's parents had legal custody of her daughter and he was afraid to ask her why.

The state of a person's relationship with their ex and their children can tell you volumes. Some people truly are victims and some partners turn difficult after being easygoing for a long time, but that isn't always the case. Don't believe everything they tell you and pay close attention to what is going on. These relationships have a history that you may or may not want to get tangled in. Even if your partner is a good and loving parent and a reasonable co-parent, difficulties with the children or the ex are not always easily overcome. Observe the child custody and support issues as well as how issues with the ex-partner are resolved.

If you are constantly told that they are doing things *just* to keep the ex quiet or that they can't have a relationship with their children because their ex is impossible, that is a big red flag. Usually these relationships are not revealed during the dating stage but when you start to become exclusive, you are going to see things that you might not want to acknowledge. Pay attention to them. Any former relationship that involves children is going to involve you, so understand what the dynamics are as your relationship progresses. In the beginning it's important to observe, but as time goes on you might want to give a few gentle suggestions.

A client said that her new boyfriend suddenly had his kids almost every weekend, whether taking them to soccer practice or having them spend two nights. The change came when his ex figured out he had a girlfriend. Not one to reject any time with his kids, he rationalized it to her as being a good dad. He did not think it was his ex putting up barriers to his new relationship. I suggested to her that she gently explain that she liked to go away sometimes and it would be nice if they could plan just one weekend every other month or so to do that. While he agreed to it, it never happened. Each weekend they had planned turned into a weekend he had to do something with or for the kids. After the second weekend was canceled, I suggested she let him know that if he couldn't see what was going on, she could, and if they weren't able to spend a weekend together once in a while, she didn't know how they would last as a couple. Again, he agreed with her but never acted on it. It became clear that she only had two choices: accept that they would never be able to plan a weekend together or end the relationship. While it's important to avoid running your new love's relationship with the ex, it's also important to know when it's time to interject some of your opinions. If those relationships are interfering with yours, try gentle suggestions at first and see how well or not so well they are received. If you're going to be a long-term partner, you might need to make the suggestion respectfully but forcefully the next time. If it's still not changing, you need to take note of that and make a decision.

With respect to kids and exes, it's important to observe all dynamics at play, including where you fit in and how your partner is managing relationships with exes and kids. As you did with your standards and compatibilities list, you need to determine what is and is not acceptable for you, and discuss and determine with your partner what can and cannot be changed. Observing your partner's actions rather than their words is a very important part of the process.

Time: How to Find Enough for Everyone and Yourself

Most people know how much or how little time they have to devote to a budding relationship. One of my clients had her list and in big, bold letters the first item was, "Has time for a relationship and spends quality time with their children (if they have any)." She was very busy so she understood being busy, but she did not understand people who were as busy as she or less busy than she who used their schedule as an excuse for not seeing each other. However, I have a friend who shares custody of a small child, as does her partner. They have not been seeing each other long enough to introduce the children, so they sometimes go almost two weeks without seeing each other. They've adjusted to the fact that this is how it needs to be for now and they're not ready to talk about when or how it will change. While both would like more time, they are settling for what they have for now.

Usually you want someone who wants to be with you. Period. Even the busiest people make time for relationships. You give time to those you love and you need to be put on the list as "someone you love" during the closest times. You must insist that you are not an option for someone. Love, this time around, has to be about reaching higher and being important in someone's life. Do not accept a low ranking on the list of priorities. Do not settle for someone who has their children on the low list of priorities or who expects you to put your children there. Do not settle for "get around to me when you can." Look for those that have the qualities you have high up on the list. Those are the people you want to be around.

Conversely, you do want to know that your new partner is making time for his or her children on outings with just them. If you have children, it's good to take your children out as a group with just Mom or Dad and it's also a good idea to treat each child to a night or day without the other siblings. Kids whose parents have separated or divorced enjoy the one-on-one time that being with a parent can provide. It's just about having a good time. Balancing all of this with a job and a new partner is difficult, but the kids will always remember feeling loved and special during an incredibly difficult time in their lives.

Remember to give love, attention, and affection to your children. Sometimes in the harried world of single parenthood, those things get lost. If you need help, ask for it. If you need a parenting class because you feel you are always blowing up at your kids or ignoring them, don't be embarrassed to take it. The best people can be overwhelmed by working and balancing parental responsibilities and a love life. It's important that you have your relationship with your children and your children's other parent as stable as it can be before you take on dating and relationships. Remember that your children did not ask for the breakup between you and their other parent. They may be confused and upset for a time. But if you handle things effectively and build good relationships with them as a solo parent, you may be a stronger family for it and well-suited to bring a new person into the fold when the time is right.

chapter 8

The Early Relationship: Identifying Issues and Working Them Out

Lisa, 36 / It's hard to do all the healing work, find someone you really care about, decide to be together as a couple, and then find you're simply not compatible.

Bonnie, 28 / I was pretty sure I was pretty secure only to be blown back to my life inventory by every little nuance of my boyfriend. Insecurity had been such a factor in my other relationships, I had to fix it (again) and quick. It's been hard but I chose well enough that we're working it out in a loving way.

Jeff, 32 / I don't want to be alone the rest of my life and that's a fear of mine but I have to balance that with being in the wrong relationship. Sometimes a series of short-lived relationships help build that final product.

Now that you have dated, have become exclusive, and are beginning a new relationship, it can be a lovely and exciting time. You're prepared to start your relationship with a clean slate by owning your mistakes in prior relationships and working on trouble spots in your life. You have your list, your affirmations, and your commitment to yourself that you will keep, no matter what. If you are coming from the breakup of a significant relationship, have spent time alone and have healed, have dated some and now are embarking on a new relationship, this may or may not be the long-term love you've dreamed about. So how do you know? Sometimes you can't know and other times you can.

Treat your early relationship like a stand-alone entity, separate from the time you dated and separate from permanent commitment. The early relationship is a temporary state that may or may not last. Everyone wants their early relationship to blossom into forever love, but if you allow that to weigh too heavily, you might miss the signs that this relationship is not the one for you. Everyone should welcome the opportunity to explore an early relationship with another person, again as a learning experience, but don't jump too far ahead or plan for things that may or may not happen. The early relationship is a time of getting to know each other in the safety of an exclusive commitment, but it's important to not jump ahead and start setting wedding dates. Go slow and be careful.

Remember your observation skills because they will be very important in the early relationship. Many times a new partner does not want to share everything with you until it's clear you're going to be together and will be more than just casual lovers. Some may be in protracted legal proceedings or have an outstanding financial obligation. There may be child support, custody, or visitation issues. It is not a good idea to share these things with everyone you are dating because the entire world does not need to know your business. You may also still have a few "tuck it in your pocket" observations and it's important to take note of what they are before proceeding.

Within the first few weeks of a new monogamous and committed relationship, assess your ability to be yourself in the relationship. Not the self that is falling in love and enamored by a new person, but the self that you are when you are not attached to someone. For example, many times in the blush of new love, both men and women fail to mention standing commitments, interests, or hobbies that have been put on hold for the honeymoon period of a relationship. It's important to present your true self to someone who may be a long-term partner. Does your new partner know you normally have dinner on Tuesday nights with your best friend or a Friday night poker game that you'll be wanting to get back to soon? Perhaps you met someone in the "off-season" of something you do that will affect your availability six months from now. Maybe you like to ski or golf or fish or never miss a Sunday football game. A client's grandparents have a summer cottage and she goes there with her girlfriends as many weekends as she can. One budding relationship ended dramatically when her new boyfriend became suspicious of what they were doing and accused her of being a party girl. Another man said his passion for outdoor photography was not as intense in the winter so his new girlfriend was unhappily surprised when summer came and, instead of going to the beach, he preferred to drive to the cliffs above and take photos of boats for hours. Neither of these relationships made it until the fall. It's important to let someone know who you are and what is important to you before it's an issue that leads to resentment and misunderstanding. Examples of questions to ask yourself:

Have you given up important things for this person?

Is your new partner truly aware of your schedule and obligations?

Is your new partner aware of how much time you like to spend with family, friends, interests, and hobbies?

Are you able to negotiate responsibilities and tasks?

Are you allowing your partner time for his or her schedule and obligations?

Are you each making time for your friends, hobbies, and interests?

Are you each making time for your families, separate and together?

The New Relationship:
Working It into Your Old Life

It's not necessary to go to every function together, but showing up when love is new is nice, especially if your friends and family have supported you during your breakup. You want your new love to be accepted into your circles. It's not necessary to attend every event together or to insist upon your new love's attendance at every function. Even though you may believe that "what others think of me is none of my business," you know that your family and friends are sizing up your new mate. If you have a mate who isn't as social as you, it's great that you value each other's differences. Still, some worry that their friends or family might see the solo appearance as trouble in the relationship. Since it's not the norm, people may ask about it. You can say it's not about what is wrong with your relationship, but what is right about it.

Balancing time together and time apart is easiest when it's something you each strive for from the very beginning. If you went through a bad breakup and then spent a long time alone, it's easy to fall into bad habits early on such as insisting on total togetherness. But it's important to know how your new mate will handle the occasional departure from coupledom. If your partner does not handle it well, that can be a red flag. It might be a pink flag for someone who has been cheated on before and is not sure what you're doing, where you're going, or who you're going with. One man could not tell the difference between his new girlfriend's nights out with her friends and his old girlfriend's lies about being out with her friends when she was really with an old boyfriend. If your partner seems insecure about time apart, talk about it because endless inquisition and pressure is not good for either of you. It's important to gain your partner's trust and agreement that being apart is okay. Try it a few times to see if you can make it a topic for discussion. Put things out on the table, which is how healthy and functional relationships work. If your mate seems innately jealous or you find that no amount of assurance helps, then you have a problem. It may be a relationship-ending scenario.

There's a popular saying on my blog and in *GPYB*: "You get what you put up with." It means that you have to start, in the very beginning, to build a relationship where you can truly blossom and grow as a person and as part of a loving couple. It's not a matter of this relationship being better than the last but being in a relationship that will last.

Take a Moment to Step Back and Inventory Your Relationship

Take time to step back and look as objectively as you can at your new partner at this juncture. Use your observation skills and ask yourself:

> *Are we both happy, healthy, whole individuals who are interested in a happy, healthy relationship?*
> *Does my new mate appear to have some unfinished business?*
> *Am I suddenly seeing a different person than the one I was dating?*

Is new information such as money problems, legal problems, or other problems suddenly being revealed?

Does my new partner seem jealous, controlling, dramatic, hot-tempered, possessive, or ridiculous?

Are red or pink flags suddenly appearing? Can we talk about them openly and honestly?

Does my new partner seem interested in working out disagreements in a healthy way?

Does my partner want to share responsibilities and tasks?

A client said, "His uncle told me that every time he got drunk he would be making out with some woman at the bar. I ignored this until one night I tracked him down and there he was, in the arms of another woman. He had both alcoholism issues and fidelity issues, but he was so charming and never drank around me, so how was I to know? Without his uncle's early tip, I could have been saddled with this for a long time." She had to revisit her life inventory and she said, "Uh-oh, I'm doing it again! Getting involved with a man who needs tracking down! There were some signs that he was this way as he liked to go off and drink with his buds, but he seemed pretty obnoxious the day after. I tried to ignore it and it came back to bite me." It was time to regroup and spend a little more time on observation.

Another man said he did not see his girlfriend's jealousy until they went to a college reunion and he introduced her to the woman who had been his best friend. He told her several times that he and the woman had been "best buds" over four years of college and nothing ever happened. His girlfriend didn't believe him and threw a tantrum in the car on the way home. "I didn't drop her and the jealousy just got worse and I kept explaining until one day I just had it." Another client said, "My partner was a great guy whom I met through friends. Everyone said we were perfect together and for the longest time we were. When we decided to move in together, he suddenly hated all my furniture, dictated how much television we could watch and who we could see on the weekends. Who was this person? Luckily I got out before I sold all my furniture."

The woman above who needed to talk out her partner's insecurity because he had an ex-girlfriend who cheated on him and lied about being with her girlfriends is one example of how these early issues can be overcome. In her situation, she was unclear as to why he was having such a problem with her spending time with her friends. He was more of a loner than she, but his reaction to her time away seemed severe. One weekend she mentioned she would be meeting her friends for dinner and he grew quiet. She knew it was time to bring it up and get it resolved one way or another. She told him that she really cared about him and their relationship but she needed time with her friends and he seemed inappropriately and unreasonably upset. After talking a while he confessed to her that the last woman he cared for as much as he cared for her had been cheating on him while claiming to be with her friends and he didn't want to fall hard again for someone doing the same thing. She told him she had never cheated on anyone, had been cheated on, and wouldn't do that to someone. She also told him it was important to her that she trust and be trusted. They both breathed a sigh of relief. The happy news is that many years later they are still together and happier than ever, but their early relationship could have easily been derailed.

Not every issue can be resolved with just one chat and not every issue should lead to a breakup. Most couples will fall somewhere in the middle. There are always early relationship issues that you definitely can work out, but the extreme end of the emotional spectrum should not be landing you in couples counseling before the relationship has even gotten off the ground. Relationships do not need to be difficult. If a relationship begins in a state of difficulty and proceeds that way, it's time to decide whether you should be going to counseling together or bailing early. Some people say they are so in love, they take the good with the bad, but that should be a conscious decision and not a fallback position because you don't want to leave this relationship or endure another breakup.

Many times "good" does not equal "good enough." You will undoubtedly meet many people along the way who are kind and who click with you in a way others don't. However, the click has to be across the board, not just sometimes, not just off-the-charts sexual activity, not just great conversation. Your "me" side of the list should have detailed what you want out of life and the "you" side should mesh. Many early relationships crash and burn because you suddenly realize that you want children and a home and your partner wants to get rich and travel around the world. Some of these topics can be discussed during dating but other times the topic doesn't come up until you each have decided to be in a committed relationship.

In addition to revisiting things you may have discussed while dating, review any potential trouble spots. This is a good time to recheck your standards and compatibilities list to confirm that you're not rolling back your standards for someone with whom you're newly involved. When you are dating, you may hesitate to challenge the other person's beliefs or remarks. Now that you are exclusive and committed, it's time to talk about anything you feel uneasy about. You need to see how you, as a couple, deal with conflict and disagreements. In the early relationship, it is imperative that you know you will be treated with love and respect at all times.

Incorporating Your Routine and Your Relationship

Defining a good relationship is relatively simple: it makes your life larger and better. An unhealthy one narrows it. Many an enmeshed couple will say, "We're together all the time! How could that be bad?" Both are missing the ability to be alone, to form and keep close friends, and to spend quality time with family. I know a few couples who are always together and they seem happy and inseparable, but what happens if one is run over by a bus or something happens to someone close to them that they had stopped seeing? One woman said she stopped going to family Sunday dinners after her partner found them tedious. A year or so into the relationship her parents were in a car accident and her mother, a lively and energetic woman, did not survive. The woman was crushed by the guilt of leaving her family in the last year of her mom's life. These are terrible things to consider in the early stages of love, but no one knows how long anyone we care about will be with us. If you have always gone to Sunday dinners and your partner finds them tedious, allow your partner off the hook and go alone, or compromise and go every other Sunday. Try not to abandon your standing Tuesday night coffee with your best friend or your golf game every Saturday morning.

A partner who supports your ideas but offers some perspective or plays devil's advocate is important. A partner who wants and needs you to be happy pursuing your dreams, reaching your goals and finding new things is important. The overall umbrella should be a relationship and a partner who supports and appreciates you as an individual and as a partner. The relationship should be the home base from which you launch your life, and the safe haven you return to when life is beating you senseless. If it's not that, then you need to rethink it.

Accept It, Change It, or Leave

As your new relationship grows, you may be confronted with issues both big and small. While you have a list of negotiable, nonnegotiable, and "may be negotiable for the right person," you may encounter things you haven't even thought about. Understand that there are only three possible responses to any issue within a relationship: accept it, change it, or leave. You can decide not to decide, but that's not a healthy response. You can table it for later, but for the most part these are the three you must consider to decide how to respond.

As noted in Chapter 4, there are three possible responses to any situation: accept it, change it, or leave. Most people will first attempt "change." Usually a smart choice, you can speak with your partner about what is bothering you, make suggestions, and perhaps even broach the idea of counseling if the issue is serious. If you are sincere about working things out in a relationship but something needs to change, it's imperative to be honest along the way. You must be honest with yourself if this issue can change; if your partner is willing to change; or if you can change it. There are some things about some people that cannot be changed. There are also people who assure you they will change and then they don't. Therefore, before you try to change a situation, you must go back to boundaries and remember the three-time rule. If you have asked someone for something three times and it hasn't changed, you are bargaining with yourself. All healthy relationships require two healthy people. For you to maintain your emotional health, you must maintain boundaries and adhere to the three-time rule for things that are important to you.

Sometimes you have to attempt change a few times before opting for leaving. A client was working toward her degree in psychology and very happy about the decision to return to school. In a course called Critical Thinking she was partnered with a man who was an engineering major. Throughout their partnership, they joked with each other about the way a therapist versus an engineer would approach each of the problems. By the end of the semester they were spending a lot of time together and eventually started dating. As all couples do, they had some disagreements and he would say to her, "You're supposed to be a therapist, you should know that people sometimes . . ." Whenever he was behaving in a way that she had a problem with, she'd let it go to avoid the "therapist" label. But one day he accused her of using "therapist skills" to manipulate him. Despite her objections, he continually accused her of this. She became exasperated and finally decided to call it quits. He wouldn't listen to her and kept using something she was happy about (being in school for something she loved) against her. Many of her friends thought the relationship was workable, but to her it was not. You need to decide for yourself if you can work with something or if someone is not willing to change something you need to change.

Sometimes a bit of investigation is necessary before deciding to leave. Another client said his new girlfriend seemed demanding. When asked to describe it, he said there was a night when she didn't seem happy with the theater tickets he bought or the restaurant where he made reservations. He had just gotten out of a long relationship with a very demanding woman who started the relationship in much the same way—being quietly upset over choices he made. An old expression is, "When all you have is a hammer, everything looks like a nail." That can describe people coming from a difficult relationship followed by a painful breakup. Sometimes your world is colored by the experience you've just had.

And so it was with him. The next time she seemed demanding, he inquired if she was unhappy with the choices he made. She seemed startled that he was asking and she reassured him that she was perfectly fine with everything. He said that he had a little bit of insecurity and she confessed she was sometimes a bit of a "tough read." He stopped projecting negativity onto her and she increased her outward enthusiasm toward his planned outings. Each worked a bit to change for the good of the relationship and this couple's "change" worked.

Accept It

Perhaps you are in a situation and you aren't sure if it's a "leave" or "change" issue. It may very well be an "accept it" issue. Look at your situation and realize that, despite your efforts, it is not changing. People may tell you to leave, but perhaps you're not ready. If that is the case, you must come to terms with "this is how it is and how it will continue to be." You can always change your mind and leave, but some people try hard to accept it first.

The problem with accepting unacceptable behavior is that it begins to erode you as a person. You have been through a devastating breakup, rebuilt your life, and found some peace. Now here is a person who is behaving in ways that you simply know, in your heart of hearts, are not okay. Accepting unacceptable behavior narrows your life. If your partner is acting in a way that is difficult for you to handle, you may start lying to your friends and family, avoid social engagements, or hide things from your children. You're back in old behaviors, doing old things, for all the wrong reasons. Keep checking in with yourself in an early relationship to figure out if things are going well and if your life is staying the same, becoming larger, or starting to narrow. Whenever we have to hide the truth from the people closest to us, our life starts to narrow.

Accepting someone's inability to quit smoking is different from accepting someone's illicit drug use or gambling addiction. Accepting someone who constantly forgets the one thing you needed from the store is different from accepting someone who doesn't come home at night. Accepting the way someone hangs the toilet paper roll is different from accepting being called names or constantly criticized or put down. Accepting someone who spends Sunday on the couch vegging out when you want to go for a walk is different from accepting someone playing you for a fool.

It is time to revisit your negotiables list and find out if this new person's behavior is or is not. The first question to ask is, *What happens to my life if I accept this behavior?* If the answer is, Nothing much, then there is no issue. If however, you are going to see a big change, you want to think about what that says for future success.

If you think something is going to change and you accept it "for now," how long will "for now" last? After two years of seeing each other and enduring a long commute, a client and her boyfriend discussed moving in together. He seemed to be looking at apartments and she made appointments and found a few good ones. But he found something wrong with each one. Finally he explained that he was comfortable where he was. Instead of walking out, she bargained with herself and decided to float the idea of her moving in with him. He needed to "make room," but months passed and he failed to do so. He stalled, she denied that was what he was doing, and capitulated year after year. If you are willing to accept something "for now," you must decide how long it's for and what you're going to do if it doesn't change.

You know you're bargaining with yourself if you hide your trouble from others or if you downplay it or rationalize it. (For example: It's not that bad. All relationships have issues. All couples go through difficult times. We're working things out.) When you bargain with yourself, nothing is as good as it could be and you pay a price for it. You enter into an unspoken, unacknowledged agreement with yourself to keep part of your life out of the light of day or away from self-examination. It's a way of holding on and not making a decision even though you know it's not changing. This is not a position you want to be in.

Leave

Leaving is always difficult if you've come off a breakup and now are face-to-face with another breakup early in a relationship that held promise. However, if you've tried to change it and cannot and tried to accept it and cannot, then it is time to leave.

Your goal is to have a healthy and happy life. We all go through life facing challenges and overcoming adversity, but we can learn to maintain balance and sanity if we have a partner who enhances our life, not one who makes it more difficult.

Your decision to leave may come after countless arguments, counseling that is not progressing, or a final blow-up. It's never fun to be in the place where you must make the decision to go.

Leaving is never 100 percent certain, even in abusive situations. The mind plays tricks and you think, "Maybe it will change." Even when you are bargaining with yourself, when you are accepting unacceptable behavior, when you are not receiving the care and love you thought you were signing up for, it's still tough to leave. Your thoughts go back to when the relationship was new. You think about how special you felt and how many compliments you received from your partner. That's nice, but you would not be falling for someone so hard if nice things did not happen at the start. The care and affection hold your attention and you enjoy feeling "this way" again. Who doesn't like falling in love again after being so miserable after that last breakup?

However, one of the goals of the inventories and exercises outlined earlier (and in *GPYB*) is for you to step back and see the relationship for what it is, not what you want it to be. The inventories are designed to help you take an objective look at the relationship as a whole. People in bad relationships tend to survive by engaging in *splitting*, which is the mental-magician trick of splitting a person into good and bad qualities, and being so in love with the good qualities that they try to dismiss the bad qualities as aberrations, as a phase, or as something that will just go away. The inventories help combat the splitting by placing good and bad qualities of your partner and of the relationship concretely in front of you.

When someone starts out special and then engages in unloving behavior, you may be hard-pressed to make sense of it. Nothing adds up. In your mind, you hold onto the parts you love, while ignoring the whole person, because the whole does not make sense to you anymore. *How can a person say X and do Y?* You tell yourself this new behavior is not the "real" person; the one you fell in love with is the "real" person. Nevertheless, the person you fell in love with does not exist. It is time to accept the facts: the relationship that held so much promise is a sham and the person you have fallen for is not the complete story.

A client had been with a woman who belittled his sexual prowess. She didn't do it often, but he felt bad for days when she did. On one of their many breakups (usually initiated by her) he met a woman who was affectionate and complimentary. They became friends and then started dating. After they became physical, she continued to shower him with affection, attention, and compliments. Because of his previous experience, he basked in it.

After six months of dating, she was suddenly pushing him to move closer to her. His job and his children were close to where he lived, and he suggested that she move closer to him. Whenever he rejected a request from her, she would withdraw physically and emotionally. He kept thinking of her as the woman who had brought him back to feeling good about himself, and it was a long time before he managed to see her as someone who bestowed affection when she felt good about things and withdrew it when she did not. He became caught up in trying to win her affection and good cheer before finally having enough.

When you are being manipulated, you sense it on one level and sooner or later you have to do something about it.

Another client left a decades-long dysfunctional marriage and didn't date for almost five years. She met a man through mutual friends and they hit it off immediately. For two years, they traveled and went to the theater together. They ate out and regularly enjoyed sporting events and concerts. After being in a very difficult marriage and then raising children by herself, the relationship was everything that she could want it to be. However, her partner started to slow down and pull away. They never went anywhere and he barely spoke to her. In the early days he mentioned to her that most of his relationships lasted about three years. It never occurred to her that this could be why. He seemed to grow weary of someone and pull away, forcing his partners to make the decision to leave, which she eventually did, but not before wasting two more years waiting for the fun, happy guy to "come back." He was never coming back. However, she endured one of the less obvious downward spirals that many people experience. Others find themselves in a relationship with someone who is verbally abusive or unfaithful or commitment-phobic. These situations are often hard to leave because you can't line up the person who whispered sweet nothings with the one who is now calling you every name in the book. It's even worse when that person is blaming you for how they are acting or why the relationship has disintegrated.

The person you are seeing now is the real person, and if that is *not* okay for you, be honest. Many people think they need to change and be more accepting or less this or less that, but sometimes it's your partner who is no longer someone who is treating you as you should be treated. Accepting that is hard. Romanticizing someone and ignoring all the ways the relationship is failing you is easy. When love is new and you want it to be "the one," it's hard to stop splitting, but it's a necessary step if you want to find real love.

The full relationship inventory is in *Getting Past Your Breakup*, but you can do a partial inventory, during a relationship, to step back and try to find some objectivity around what is going on. Take a piece of paper and write down all the positive aspects of the person on one side and all the negative aspects on the other side. Write down five special things your partner did for you. Write down the five worst things.

Take a few days away from your mini relationship inventory and let it settle. Come back and work on seeing the person as a whole—good, bad, and indifferent. Is this the person you want to share your life with? If not, it's okay to leave. You need to do what is best for you and your life. It's important to grieve the good person while acknowledging the hurtful person as well. They are one and the same; be glad that neither is still in your life.

Examples of Specific Early Relationship Issues

Early in a relationship, people tend to ignore simple things. When you are busy looking at the big picture, you lose your sense or excuse small things. Go back to basics. Now that the honeymoon is over, the truth about a person comes through.

Here are some common issues that show up early on in many relationships.

Basic Decency

Consider if your new love shows common decency and basic politeness. It is not necessarily the way they speak to you, but how they speak to others. Listen for snide remarks and comments that may hint at a jealous or controlling personality. When you're in a new relationship and someone makes an offhand remark to bring you down, you must take note of it (and, unless it is truly egregious, tuck it in your pocket). If it is egregious, then you need to make an "accept it, change it, or leave" decision.

A client traveled frequently with his girlfriend. He liked traveling with a companion and didn't mind paying all the expenses. He wanted each trip to be special, but whenever they arrived, she would criticize the hotel room, the rental car, the way he conducted himself, the food, or the people in general. When the trip was over, she never said "thank you," she never said "I love you," and she never said "I'll miss you" when they parted after a long trip. He was the one who always said it and nothing but silence came back on the other end. Basic decency and common courtesy dictate that you say "thank you" to a person who takes you on a nice trip. It also dictates that you don't complain about everything. When I suggested that he should have set a boundary on her complaining, he said she was the type to say, "Good. Don't take me anywhere." He felt there was no way to win with her, and when it came down to "accept it, change it, or leave," he left.

Through Thick and Thin

When looking for a partner in life, what you want is somebody who will be there at 2:00 in the morning when the baby is vomiting, the dog wants to go out but is afraid of the torrential downpour, and the roof is leaking. You need someone to say, "Don't worry, you call the pediatrician while I get an umbrella and take Fido outside." Then one of you gets a bucket for the leak. There is no hostility, no anger, no blaming, and no complaining.

Life is what it is and sometimes it's rough. You need someone to support you, to let you know things will be okay. It is important to find a true partner who will help you with life's challenges and down times. A client loves her dog and says he has a "charming personality and looks like a little lion." He really does. They go for long walks and when she feels lonely, she takes him out to the park or to a dog-friendly coffee shop. When dating, she started to look at men and think, "Will he help me take my dog to the vet at 2:00 AM?" It's not always easy to "size someone up" as the one who will be there when your pooch needs to see a doctor in the middle of the night, but it is easier to recognize those who won't.

Habits

It's important to have similar values and to discuss those that seem opposite. A client started to date a guy who was in her social group. They had known each other socially for almost a year and liked each other. When they started to date, the rest of the social circle pronounced them "the cutest couple in the world." They were flattered and happy at how well they got along. Being in a social group helped in one way, but as they grew to know each other as boyfriend and girlfriend, he confessed that he smoked a lot of pot. Having preteens, she told him that was not acceptable. They could continue to see each other, but there was no future that would involve moving in. "I can't tell my kids it's not okay to do drugs if my boyfriend is smoking pot every night. My kids are not stupid." His best friend told him that she was controlling and ridiculous about it and he, mistakenly, conveyed that information to his girlfriend. A huge argument ensued. She said, "I am not trying to control you, I'm telling you the standards I have for my life and my house. I will continue to see you, to be in a committed relationship, but until my kids are all grown and out of the house (in about ten years) I won't move in with you if you smoke pot every night."

About six months after they were seeing each other, they struck a bargain where he would smoke now and again away with his friends. He had been with her almost every night anyway and didn't even feel like smoking pot when he got home or when he stayed over. "It was a thing my friends did every night and I did it too. I didn't think much about it, but I suppose I can't live in house full of teens and be with their mom who is anti-drug if I'm doing it every night." Eventually he stopped altogether, but it took patience and compassion on each end for them to find their "happily ever after."

Caustic Emotions

Early in the relationship look for common courtesy, lack of blaming, and how someone reacts when you ask for basic things such as acknowledging a nice gesture, bringing something home, or helping out around the house. If someone becomes habitually unglued or angry over life's many trials and tribulations, you want to know that because it's a very important thing. It's not just about keeping your head when all about you are losing theirs, but that you're both keeping your heads when things around you are blowing up and your mission is to safeguard each other. A friend of mine said her husband worked himself up over a door that was giving him a lot of trouble. Having been with a rage-aholic in her previous relationship, she began to panic as he grew angry over the door. Finally he let out a growl, and she had to step back as he took the door outside and flung it over the deck into the yard. Gingerly she stepped out to offer some help, nervous that he was going to start screaming at her as her last partner had. He turned to her and, hands on hips, said, "Well, I taught that door, now didn't I?" and he let out a laugh. She let out a sigh of relief and then a laugh. Whenever he felt upset or angry like that, he was able to let it go and laugh at it. It took her some time to realize he was not her former partner; he had a much better sense of humor and controlled his anger.

Walks in the Moonlight Are Nice, but What About Chores?

A long-term consideration is the ability to negotiate tasks and responsibilities such as household chores and child care duties. Successful couples discuss these issues and have them ironed out before moving in together or having children so it's not a daily or long-running disagreement or problem. While it's premature in the early relationship to allocate household chores, it's not premature to assess your mate's ability to negotiate a framework for ongoing tasks and responsibilities before you get too deeply involved. This goes back to Chapter 2: observe, gather information, and then tuck it away. It's very easy to be caught up in a new relationship and ignore the potential long-term hazards.

Be Honest with Yourself

Some are reluctant to leave a relationship in the early stages because they've already invested time in it, or they don't want to be alone again. They remember the bumps they experienced in dating, whether one of the five Rs or something else, that makes them reluctant to imagine themselves back on the dating scene. That fear can keep people stuck for years: "I've invested six months, a year, two years, three years [whatever], and I don't want to walk now." Well, if you don't walk, you're just going to invest five more years, ten more years, twenty more years, into the same old thing. It's like throwing good money after bad. It's not going to get better and every client I've ever had can describe an early time or incident where they should have walked. One client described a horrific experience where he was literally chasing his girlfriend through the small town they lived in. So thoroughly caught up in trying to find her, he had no clue what he was doing. Drama was the hallmark of their relationship for the following two years. Even though that day happened early on, he said, "That's the day I should have gone and I didn't." A day doesn't have to be that nutty for you to pay attention to it. In every early relationship, keep your standards, boundaries, and negotiable list in your head. Do not bargain with yourself or compromise for another's affection. Remember it is better to be alone than to settle for less or to put up with crazy nonsense. Ask yourself if you've come this far only to start bargaining with yourself again.

Be careful not to start making excuses for a new partner. If you are telling people how busy your partner is at work but secretly know that you're not receiving the attention you deserve, there is a problem. If you are bargaining with yourself early on, regarding how much love and attention you need and deserve, you are going to be doing that for a long time to come. If you abandon yourself, others will too. Stay strong in your commitment to yourself and insist that others do as well.

Communication Styles: Separately and Together

The next chapter will deal in depth about communication styles in lasting relationships, but for now, it's important to take note of your communication style and method of dealing with disagreements in early relationships and know that it might need some tweaking. You and your partner both have rights, such as the right to be quiet, to be crazy, to be obstinate, and to say nothing. You both have the right to not put up with behaviors that are going to trigger your feeling of craziness or being out of control, and your partner has a right to not put up with behaviors that will trigger them into feeling out of control. It's not that healthy couples never have these crazy-inducing arguments, but it's important to recognize them and to talk it out when there is no anger and no emotional upheaval. For couples who have been in unhealthy relationships, turning arguments into learning and growth experiences can be difficult. Early in your relationship you want to know that you can do that; neither of you is perfect. Understanding flaws, triggers, and things that set you off is a start. A twofold process is that you continue to work on your flaws, triggers, and what sets you off while letting your partner know that a certain thing is hard for you to deal with right now. Being understanding and reasonable is the key to working these out.

Sometimes going to separate corners helps you understand what is happening. Sometimes you must disengage emotionally and keep up the positive self-talk that you are a healthy person seeking healthy relationships and you need to find what is causing this drama. As always, give yourself credit for being healthy enough to want to get things right. Leaving a new relationship does not make you a failure, but rather someone who is learning how to be a good partner with a compatible person. Often the early times in a relationship tell us that we are not ready yet. It doesn't mean you never will be, but that there is someone better for you. There is. Trust your process.

If your early relationship is working well, good for both of you! It's not easy to navigate relationships and if you are managing well, that is wonderful news. Every relationship can use a "couples inventory." It is like a life inventory that you work on together. If your early relationship appears to be working out, get ready to make the next list!

chapter 9

The Couples List of Standards for a Healthy Relationship: Communication, Compromise, and Compassion

Jenn, 32 / My first standard was that I would never let anyone call me names again. When I announced this to my husband on our third date, I could tell by the way he looked at me that it was something I didn't need to worry about.

Brian, 37 / I was always willing to compromise but found I gravitated to those who didn't. I thought I could win some kind of prize if I got someone who was difficult to work with me. That was a problem I had with my father and when I recognized it, I was able to stop looking for it. When I started to look for compromise in who I dated and early in relationships, I actually found it.

Jeremy, 26 / It seems as if everyone from my parents to my co-workers were very rude to me. When I started setting boundaries and insisting that I be spoken to with care, it wasn't easy but practice brought new and healthy people into my life.

Rhonda, 49 / I have always been a bit heavy-handed with my opinion, to say the least. When I stepped back to listen to my partner and care what he was talking about, things became decidedly better.

Gretchen, 44 / We were in a definite honeymoon period for the first year. Then he started to have periods where he disappeared and even one where he seemed unsure he wanted to be together. I pulled away to give him time to think, but I knew I couldn't go through much more of this. When we came back together, we had to sit down and figure out what kind of couple we were going to be and what that was going to look like. I couldn't keep worrying that everything I said or did was going to scare him off.

Many times relationships sink or swim based on the 3 Cs: communication, compromise, and compassion. I have counseled couples, gay and straight, old and young, in the relationship a long time and in the relationship a short time, and most problems come down to one of the 3 Cs. If there are other issues, such as unresolved issues from childhood, these can be revisited in your life inventory. Sometimes revisiting an issue and taking responsibility for relapsing into old patterns can be a boon to your participation in creating the very important "couples list of standards for a healthy relationship."

The Couples List of Standards for a Healthy Relationship

A good relationship is both a springboard to launch your life and a fortress in the storm. Longtime couples often forget these important functions of their relationship. One way to remember it is to work together on the couples list of standards. Just as you made a list of standards for yourself when you were single, it helps to make a list of standards for your committed relationship that you adhere to, no matter what. As mentioned in the last chapter, long-term success often depends on the ability to have things worked out and agreed on to avoid day-to-day arguments. Sometimes couples don't notice the things that drive them crazy until they move in together. There may need to be a period of hashing it out. Other times there is a slow, downward slide into dysfunction that may not even be recognized. Sometimes couples enter a period of not getting along, and they are unsure if this means the end or is just a bump in the road.

Like the woman whose partner disappeared every now and again after the initial honeymoon period, it's important to sit down and hash out what kind of couple you're going to be and decide if that works for each of you. Sometimes it will and sometimes it won't. While adjusting to each other can take some time, your relationship should be a work in progress moving in a direction you agree on. Often a couple has a bumpy period after the initial honeymoon phase because they don't talk about what kind of couple they are going to be. It might seem unromantic or scary, but not doing so can lead to a lot of misunderstandings and even a breakup that didn't have to happen. It's important, as you enter the commitment phase of a relationship, that you sit down and talk about what you each need as an individual and what you'd like to see you become as a couple.

Whether early on or later, many times life gets in the way and when children, houses, pets, and the like come along, a couple can find themselves snapping at each other in a way they never did before. If a child is sick or a family member passes, couples may not know how to meet these challenges. It's important to have a foundation that you always return to when times are tough. Your list is the key to that foundation.

Many people balk at sitting down and making an actual list, and if you prefer to just talk it out, that's okay. But having something concrete to refer to can be helpful. There can be disagreements later on where one person says, "I never agreed to that." It's not to throw it in someone's face, "Yes, you did! Look at this list!" but to gently remind them of what you agreed to as a couple. If things are going well, many people don't want to introduce the idea of making a list, but the list can evolve out of early growing pains and "hashing it out" conversations that many couples need to have. It may be during a bump in the road or a decision to be exclusive and monogamous, but a conversation—or series of conversations—about "what kind of couple are we going to be?" should take place.

The sections below address items that should be on your couples list.

The Big Picture

The overriding standards for a healthy relationship include:

- Love, respect, and trust are actions and not just words.
- The sun doesn't have to be shining for me to shine my love on you.
- When things go wrong, we grow closer, not farther apart.
- We love each other and act that way, under any circumstance.
- The worse the circumstance, the closer we stand to each other.
- Differences over small things can be worked out in a civil, loving way.
- We care about each other's feelings and concerns.
- We work to find the solution right for us as individuals and as a couple.

As a new couple, discuss the big picture items. During times of stress you may need to breathe in and out, count to ten, and recall the big picture items. Sometimes just reminding yourself, "The sun does not have to be shining for me to shine my love on my partner," will make the difference between trying to work things out and storming out of the room. What other things are big picture items for your relationship?

Healthy Communication for a Lasting Love

The biggest issue in many relationships is communication. Happy couples have good communication and unhappy ones do not. Healthy couples may know that the silent treatment, barking at the one you love after a long day of work, or stomping off during an argument is not functional behavior, but that doesn't mean it never happens. While no one is perfect, a list of guidelines for communication on the couples list will be helpful when the urge to ice up, bark, or stomp comes along.

In healthy relationships, there must be an atmosphere of mutual love, trust, respect, care, and concern. These conditions do not exist if a couple is arguing endlessly, becoming blinded by anger, or becoming caught up in their partner's behavior without looking at their own. Once those cracks appear in the relationship and you are both off to the races, there is usually little, short of intense counseling, that can bring you back. Therefore, before either of you acts out in an unloving manner toward the other, it's important to understand and agree on ground rules.

The Role of Constructive Criticism and "I" Language

A standard for healthy couples is to use "I" language. This is one of the most important communication skills to learn and benefits you in all situations, but especially on the home front. If, during an argument, one of the first three words out of your mouth is "you," it can be more hurtful than helpful. It's not just your partner who suffers, but you do also because "you" often leaves your partner on the defensive rather than in a position to listen to what you have to say. Communication should be helpful and not harmful to the relationship. If the communication is helpful but the behavior continues, a boundary may have to be set.

Another way to ask for things or to constructively criticize arises when you are discussing your feelings. You might feel put upon, as if you do more than everyone else and that is making you upset. If you say, "I feel as if the chores are unbalanced around here," you are talking about your feelings and no one can say, "Well, don't feel that way!" especially if you follow up with, "And I'd like to talk about how we can change that." Not once have you said "you" or attacked anyone in any way.

Healthy couples communicate by giving thoughtful, constructive criticism to express their thoughts and feelings without placing blame or guilt on the other party. It's a matter of keeping the parameters of the conversation as clear as possible. If one partner has difficulty expressing thoughts and feelings, it's good to write them down and read them or, as a last resort, send in an email.

EXAMPLES	
Unhelpful Communication	Helpful Communication
1. You never put your clothes in the dryer when you do the wash. You make me really angry when you do this! (This client actually threw the wet clothes on the floor in frustration and the ensuing argument lasted for hours.)	1. I would appreciate it if you put the clothes in the dryer as soon as they're done in the washer so I can do my own wash.
2. You never pick up Emma on Tuesdays after her band practice like you said you would. You're going to make me get fired for leaving work early every Tuesday!	2. I would appreciate it if you pick up Emma on Tuesdays as we agreed you would. I think my boss is getting annoyed that I'm leaving early every Tuesday.
3. You drive like a maniac. You're trying to get us killed. If you don't slow down, I'm never riding with you again.	3. I get really scared when you drive 20 miles over the speed limit and weave in and out of cars. I would like to drive if you can't slow down or keep a safe distance from the other cars.

Texting

Texting has become epidemic, but it's not always a good thing. It can be lazy communication and has only a small place in important relationships. It's great for reminding someone to pick up an item at the store and even in some silly, fun discoveries early on, but should not be something a couple engages in too much and never for an important conversation. Whenever you are upset with each other or are having an argument, avoid texting.

Texting may be a habit you have gotten into with friends and family and with your partner early on. It's important to break the habit of discussing important things with anyone in text messages as feelings are hurt with texts and emails that probably wouldn't be hurt via a phone or in-person conversation. If you're in the habit of texting with your partner, you will each benefit from scaling back. Saying things by text is easier than on the phone or in person, so be careful not to ask questions you don't want the answer to. End texting early.

Part of learning to be in loving relationships is to learn to let go of disagreements and dismay with your partner. Carrying around hostile exchanges all day and reading them or showing them to every person you know is not going to help anyone get over anything. Avoid the temptation to engage in text wars. Make a commitment to yourself and others that nothing important will be discussed or debated over text. Your life will change for the better.

It's also important to spend time together without the phones. If you've ever sat in a restaurant, you've noticed couples or even entire families with their phones out looking at them instead of each other. New studies show that people who unplug and spend time talking to each other are happier than those who don't. Take time to listen to each other and time to just be together. If you have to place a moratorium on phone usage, whether at dinner or after a certain hour, do it. It's hard at first as we've all gotten so used to it, but you will be happy you did.

If you're waiting in line together, take the time to talk instead of staring at your phone. When Michael and I went to get our marriage license at City Hall in Manhattan, we were dismayed to find the line snaking out into the hall. If we had smartphones at the time, I don't doubt we would have pulled them out. Instead, we were entertained by the goings-on in the marriage license office. Between the beleaguered clerks and the mountains of confusing paperwork, the stage was set for several comical vignettes as we waited. We had such a good time watching and laughing that we were almost sorry when it was over. For years we took great pleasure in repeating stories from that day. A few weeks ago I was in line at the deli and a young couple was in front of me. They were each surfing on their phones. She finished and put hers away and tugged at his arm. He shooed her away. I felt sad for both of them and couldn't help but think back to the day in the marriage license bureau, thankful there were no smartphones then. Take time to put the phones away and talk to each other and observe what is going on around you even if it's waiting in line at the deli. Even if not much happens, it's the ability to withstand boredom and spend it together that will help you grow stronger as a couple.

Does This Need to Be Said?

Couples will disagree with each other. However, not every disagreement needs to be aired and not everything that your partner does needs a comment from you. One of the clearest guidelines I've ever heard was from Craig Ferguson, who said after three marriages he's learned to ask himself:

> *Does this need to be said?*
> *Does this need to be said by me?*
> *Does this need to be said by me now?*

On the couples list, include these three important questions. It's important to know whether or not now is the time, this is the topic, and I am the person to say this. It's hard to stop and think about the answers to these questions when you're lost in the rapid-fire mode of text arguments. On your couples list, I absolutely believe you should address the issue of electronic communication even if you need to use your device to make the couples list! (Ironic, isn't it?) Many disagreements only get worse in text and email, and many issues can be resolved by picking up the phone. The longer you go without picking up the phone or talking in person, the worse it can be. As soon as things seem to be getting heated or confused, pick up the phone or see each other as soon as you can.

Many times a couple can benefit by stepping back and cooling off. It's hard to make this happen if you're texting. Sometimes you need to just let things go. Giving up control helps most couples come out on the other side lovingly intact. If someone has a power and control issue or one is not picking up slack that needs to be picked up, it will become abundantly clear soon enough without any words being exchanged. If someone is hurt or angry but confused about why, sitting down and trying to write it out by yourself will help.

It's not just texting that can be problematic. Sometimes partners have different ways of arguing. In fact people are often drawn to someone who is opposite in temperament and negotiation style. That is wonderful when love is new, but can be problematic later on. One person wants to talk until everything is settled and the other wants to ignore the issue. It's important that both styles are recognized and each gives a little in recognition of the other's preference. Therefore it's good to set a time limit on a cooling off period as well as the time to come back together to talk. That way someone who is feeling angry and aggrieved and wants to talk knows the time will come when you will talk, and the person who just wants to ignore the whole thing knows there will be a respite from the heated argument.

When both parties come back to the issue, it is helpful to have time limits for each to speak and it is not unhelpful for each to have an outline of points they'd like to make. Perhaps not every argument will result in clear disposition of the problem or issue, and there may need to be several conversations, but the goal is to work toward resolution without extracting a pound of emotional flesh from each other.

Many times if you ask and answer the Craig Ferguson questions, the answer to one of those three questions is clearly no. Prattling on about nothing or a small item is tantamount to destroying a relationship little by little. You may have a partner who ignores these sorts of seemingly inane things for the most part, but eventually even the most easygoing person is going to feel weighted down by criticism and complaints. If you add other things, such as a frequent foul mood, name-calling, or the silent treatment, to these sorts of nitpicking monologues, the relationship will either end or you both will be miserable for a very long time.

Neutrality in Talking Things Out

One of the important items on the couples list should be discussing repetitive arguments or differing styles at a time when things are not heated and there is no grudge or anger in the air. It's hard to work out fair compromises and helpful solutions when you're angry or hurt. Your perspective is important, and that is at its best when your emotions are not running high. Couple check-ins are important, but don't overdo it. Sometimes learning to let go of a heated exchange is healthier than revisiting it. Revisiting it is usually necessary for areas of contention or repetitive arguments that are getting on both partners' nerves. Some examples:

1. Polar Opposites When Stressed

Life is stressful. As couples pay more attention to the outside world than to each other, they may find it's too late to do anything about their different styles. Sometimes when one partner is stressed, another room away from everyone is the place to be. The other partner may want to draw near and talk until dawn. When love is new, it may be awkward to ask, "What is your 'I've had a bad day' preference?" If this doesn't happen in the beginning, it can be discussed when it arises. In the case of polar opposites, especially where stress is concerned, compromise is important. The person who wants to retreat for hours may have to say to the person who wants to talk, "Give me an hour to cool down and collect my thoughts and then we'll talk for an hour." This is a compromise that's easy to see from the outside, but not so easy when you're in it. When styles are this different, couples need to discuss, when things are not heated, how to tackle this problem.

Sometimes when you have a bad day, you just want someone to listen. Sometimes you may want to hear what they think or if they have a solution. As a caring partner, you may ask,

"Is there something you want me to do about this or do you just want me to listen?" So many communication problems are solved by *asking* what your partner needs and by not expecting them to know automatically what you need. Do not expect to be or have to be a mind reader. Discuss together and listen to each other.

2. Teacher/Student

Partners react badly to being lectured or talked down to, though often the lecturer does not realize it. A way to communicate this to your mate is, "I feel like an errant child when you go on and on like that. I understood your point the first time you said it, and would appreciate it if we can drop it now." This can be dicey territory, but again, if you strive to be a healthy couple, these things have to be said and worked out. Many times someone is not being malicious or stubborn but just communicates differently than you're comfortable with. However, in all things, check your own sensitivity and insecurity. Sometimes your partner can help the relationship by pulling back on the lecturing as you pull back on your sensitivity. A couple can have an honest discussion about this issue and agree to a time limit for driving home a point. This can help avoid someone yelling, "OKAY, I HEARD YOU, I GET IT!" or simply glazing over until the prattling partner stops repeating what was said six hours ago.

3. Always and Never Should Always Never Happen

Another list item is avoiding the words "always" and "never" in arguments, such as, "You always leave everything out, you leave the laundry on the pool table and the milk on the counter and you never listen to me when I ask you to put things away." Another thing to avoid is tying small annoyances to how your partner feels about you: "You don't love me. If you did, you'd stop doing these things that drive me crazy." These are easy traps to fall into and may seem to be nothing more than statements said in the heat of the moment, but they can pile up and turn into resentments. For more on this, see "Never Resolving the Issue" below.

4. Zingers

Even during times of anger, there should be no name-calling, no bringing up the past, and no zingers. Play fair and fight fair. Have ground rules for disagreements. Otherwise when anger flares, you may find yourself having disagreements that are hellish hours of having your words twisted, overly explaining or defending yourself, or being spoken to in a very disrespectful manner—or you may find yourself behaving that way. Don't brush away your hurtful language with, "I was only playing!" or "You can't take a joke!" If your partner doesn't like a word, a phrase, or a "joke," it's not okay to use it. If a certain word or label triggers your partner's sensitivity, don't use it. Hitting below the belt is never okay and using words your partner is sensitive to is exactly that.

5. "End of Convo"

In addition to disagreeing in a respectful manner, you also need to have discussions. Being with someone who refuses to discuss things, by stating something like, "I don't want to argue about this," is very frustrating and leads nowhere. One client said her husband would get the last word in and announce, "End of convo!" There was nothing she could say to pull him back into the discussion. Another client complained that her mate always shut off conversation at 11:00 PM by saying, "I can't resolve anything after eleven. I need my sleep." But in the morning he would announce that last night's discussion was off-limits.

Nothing can be resolved if it's not okay to talk about it. It's hard to let someone go just because you have differing argumentation styles, but sometimes it may be necessary. All couples need to be able to talk about differences and how to resolve them and keep the relationship strong. Without that component, a relationship will wither and die. If your communication styles are very different and one person always sets a time limit or gets sick of the argument, it's helpful to allow each person to (1) air grievances using "I" language and (2) suggest changes to the situation. After that, suggest a compromise or if the problem is unsolvable, one person may need to draw a boundary. But when the conversation ends, both partners must have been heard. If the issue is not resolved within a certain preset time period, set a day and time to revisit it and, again, agree on how long you're going to talk about it.

6. Never Resolving the Issue

Another problem, like "always" and "never," is chronic failure to resolve issues. Sometimes it's not one partner who refuses to revisit and resolve once and for all, but both. They conspire together to have a blowup and then make up without ever resolving the disagreement. The disagreement comes up again and again. The couple eventually begins to complain about going in circles—because they are. Even if you need a therapist to help with a single issue, better to visit for one issue than to let it fester and undermine the relationship.

Another list item is avoiding assigning intent, thoughts, or hurt to issues. Perhaps you've said something like, "You don't love me because you keep leaving the milk out," knowing that is not the case. If you truly believe that someone is not respecting your reasonable wishes, like putting the milk back in the refrigerator because that will reduce the grocery bill, it's time to sit down and talk about it and not assume they don't love you.

A good way to start is, "Honey [or whatever nickname you have for your partner], I'm concerned about the fact that you're still leaving the milk out after I've asked you not to numerous times. Is this a way to tell me that you don't love me anymore?" Your partner may respond with, "That's ridiculous! I'm just forgetful." Or "I feel like you're controlling me and I don't like it." Or "Oh no honey. If my leaving the milk out makes you feel that way, then I will do a better job of remembering to put it away. Maybe I'll put a sign on the refrigerator that says, 'Remember to put the milk away!'"

It's even okay to say, "I'm afraid and insecure over this [small reoccurring issue]," even if your partner may think you're being dramatic or silly. It's okay to say, "I feel even more insecure when you invalidate my feelings by calling them dramatic or silly."

If you're the partner who is dismissive and saying things like that, it's a good idea to simply reassure your partner and try to remember the small reoccurring issue.

7. Opinions of Third Parties Not Present

A standard for disagreements should include not bringing third parties into arguments. A woman said her husband continually quoted his twin sister, a psychologist. "If I hear 'my sister thinks' one more time, I'm going to scream. She's a psychologist but she's not *our* psychologist and I don't like him running to her with every little problem we have." That is a pitfall for many couples, even those in individual or couples counseling. They will argue about what the therapist said or meant. When I'm working with couples, I tell them not to argue about what I said or what suggestions I make unless we're in session. I also caution those I work with one-on-one with not to tell a new person in their life that I'm questioning some behavior of theirs. Sometimes they not only fail to communicate my commentary but also fail to frame it in the appropriate light or with the appropriate language. No one wants to hear, as one of my clients summed up our conversation with words I never said, "My therapist thinks you're a wacko." Certain things need to be off-limits, and "what my [best friend, mother, therapist, co-worker] thinks of you . . ." is one of those things.

8. Mind Reading

An earlier chapter mentioned a couple that broke up in part due to mind reading. One of the most destructive communication issues is saying, "I know you think . . ." but what follows has nothing to do with what the other partner is thinking. It's very harmful to get into the habit of arguing about what you're not thinking or not doing or what you didn't mean by that remark. This goes back to intent to hurt. Assigning intent or telling someone what he or she is thinking is relationship dynamite. People can only defend what they're not doing or thinking for so long. Then they get weary and move on.

Perfect People Are Imperfect

Neither you nor your partner is perfect, and you may find yourself engaging in the behaviors described above. The important thing is that both of you want the best for yourself, your partner, and the relationship. It's a tough balancing act and even the most easygoing couples can find the balance out of whack sometimes. It's good to check in with yourself and each other from time to time. In a healthy relationship, common human foibles should not turn into litmus tests of love. However, if it happens all the time, you may start to feel insecure. I usually tell my couples to include the following items on their lists for communicating:

- Don't go crazy over little things.
- Pick your battles.
- Don't be mean to each other.
- Try to hear what your partner is saying to you.
- Ask your partner, nicely, if he or she is hearing you. If you are not sure your partner is hearing you, ask him or her to repeat back what you said or what

you're asking for. Sometimes you will find it differs greatly from what you are saying.

- It is sometimes uncomfortable for one partner to say, "Tell me what you heard me say." But it's a technique used in couples counseling, and if you want to avoid couples counseling, put it on your couples list as an acceptable question to ask. Communication is a skill that can always be improved. Don't take communication issues personally.

Dysfunctional Behavior That Destroys a Relationship

Some communication styles can turn good relationships into bad relationships. One client told me that her partner would scream at her for the way she was driving and even threatened once to get out of the car, on the highway, when it was raining. Yet her partner didn't want to drive. Most of what she described in other areas told the tale of a dysfunctional relationship, but the "boxed in" scenario where there is no answer often comes up in little things rather than big things. If those little things crop up and you can't stand a lifetime of them, or if your partner relays displeasure in unhealthy ways, it's not the relationship for you.

If someone is screaming at you, you can gently say, "Please don't scream at me." I worked with one couple where the husband was ready to walk out because his wife screamed instead of talking. He was a quiet person and never really raised his voice, but the screaming became an issue after they had children. He said, "I can't take her screaming at me in front of the kids. They are young now, but I think that if it continues, they won't respect me." It was true. The wife had been raised in a house where screaming was the norm and "didn't really mean anything" in the end. She kept trying to convince him that the level of her voice didn't mean she didn't love him. It was true that she was raised in a house where screaming was acceptable and after an argument, no one held a grudge, but life was different now. It took a third party, me, to show each of them how this developed and to help them find other ways of communicating.

Not everyone is going to do everything perfectly. If someone leaves the milk out, you don't rage for seven hours and bring up everything the person ever did wrong. It's better to say, "I would appreciate it if you put the milk back in the refrigerator. Leaving it out makes it spoil sooner than it should and that costs money." You can hope that next time or the time after that, the message comes through, but sometimes it means having to live with it. You also don't get to bring up the milk when you're having a dispute about the laundry. There are other examples of dysfunctional communication behavior that has no place in healthy relationships, for example, bullying, blaming, and walking on eggshells.

Bullying and Blaming

Sometimes people can turn into bullies without realizing it. Typically it begins with blaming or scapegoating the partner, the children, or even family and friends. Noting a person's tendency to do this is important at every stage of a relationship. Though it was evident early on that her husband assigned fault no matter what happened, it became unbearable for one woman after they had children. She said, "No matter what happened, he had to find someone to blame. If one of the kids fell down it was because I wasn't watching them, not because kids fall down. If my husband ran over a bike in the driveway, it was because someone left it in his way even if it was off to the side and he could have avoided it by looking before barreling into the driveway. If a package wasn't delivered, it was because no one was listening for the doorbell, not because it was still at the shippers. If the electric bill was high, it was because we were all leaving lights on, not because the electric company sent an estimated bill. If a book of his was missing, someone took it, it wasn't that it slipped under the sofa when he fell asleep reading it. Most of the time there wasn't anyone to blame but he yelled and blamed anyway. If it turned out he was wrong, he wouldn't apologize for his rant." The tirades occurred daily and even when they went to counseling and the therapist told him to stop, he continued. He was not interested in saving the relationship but in being right even when he wasn't. His wife said, "He was so difficult to get along with and yet was completely surprised the day I left with the kids."

He may have found something in their behavior maddening, but he had become so entrenched in the blaming and bullying that he was not able to see it years later. For her part, she had allowed it to go on so long that they were both helpless to correct it after a certain point. He didn't think she'd leave, and she left because she didn't think he'd change. Someone may be to blame when things go wrong, but that is not always the case. If you're the person who sees the problem, you might ask your partner, "How can we fix the problem that the electric bill is very high every month?" rather than bellowing that someone is leaving the lights on. If you're the partner being blamed, you might say, "I know this is very aggravating to you and I've tried to make sure that the kids are more diligent about turning the lights off, but I think it's unfair not to give us credit for trying to rectify the situation." If you agree that blame and fault-finding have no place but that everyone needs to do his or her best to be responsible, these situations may be resolved early on.

Walking on Eggshells

If there is one phrase that comes up in dysfunctional or deteriorating relationships, it's "walking on eggshells." No one should have to live like that or with that. There is no reason to walk on eggshells because your partner appears to be looking for an argument every time you turn around. At the same time, it's not okay to be tethered to someone who doesn't care a whit. When one person is the only one managing things, they can become infuriated even if they don't have power and control issues. It's very easy to blow up if you feel as if you're the only grown-up living in a house. While "walking on eggshells" usually stems from one domineering and controlling partner, the attitude and lack of adult participation by the other partner needs to change before the relationship can succeed. If one partner is simply a bully and the other downtrodden and abused, they need to get into counseling or part ways so that the destructive communication can stop.

Compromise

Compromise is, as we've seen, an important list item. Finding the middle is important when you've had a bad day. If you need something that your partner does not understand (like being left alone for the rest of the night or throwing your golf clubs in the woods), explain this to your partner in a neutral moment with love, kindness, and "I" language.

You can come to a compromise that meets in the middle, such as, "When I've had a bad day, I just want to come home and be left alone." Your partner may say, "I understand that, but I feel abandoned. If you could just hug and kiss me and tell me you've had a bad day and would like some alone time, that would make me feel better." Another possible compromise is not taking the entire evening for alone time. Take an hour or two and then sit down with your partner to watch television or something that doesn't require much energy.

What do you do about meals when you've had a bad day and want to be alone? Do you sit sulking in the other room with a plate that your partner prepared? That can be construed as not fair or loving. You may have to visit your "bad day silence" and make a compromise to eat meals together and then retreat to an alone space. Coming to a compromise that involves a little give and get on both sides is what a healthy relationship looks like. Many times an issue that has the potential for a real blowup can be nipped in the bud if addressed early enough.

A list item question should be, Is there a simple solution to this? To revisit the great milk debate again, if your partner just can't remember the milk, you can introduce the idea of putting a sign on the refrigerator. If the problem is deeper than just forgetfulness, then the sign isn't going to be effective. One woman said, "I thought our issue was housecleaning, but when I hired a housekeeper, he didn't stop about all the things that were wrong. I fired several housekeepers, but the arguments continued. It was not about housecleaning at all. It was about power and control, and I needed to get out. He wouldn't be satisfied in a million years." If someone is not going to be satisfied when an obvious solution is presented, there isn't much you can do about it.

A happy medium should be the goal of all romantic relationships, with each giving some and getting some, winning some and losing some. Finding the middle and doing what you can to get there together, with give-and-take on each side, is what real love is all about. When you have kids, pets, and a job, it's easy for anyone to find something wrong. In a fast-paced world where most of us are busy or harried, it's best to avoid falling into an argument and instead propose solutions and listen for a willingness to negotiate. When each side becomes entrenched in a position, it's impossible to untangle the issues and achieve resolution.

Sometimes if you stop and try to work together toward a solution, you discover what is really going on. Perhaps, as in the bullying and blaming example above, the kids are leaving all the lights on and the vendor didn't ship the package on time. By blaming everything on everyone, the man lost a chance to fix things, and his wife and kids learned to tune him out until they simply couldn't any longer. Looking deeper into an issue will help rein in out-of-control arguing and fussing. This couple divorced and he remarried someone who cared more about the house and electric bills and she remarried someone who cared less. They each went toward what they said they wanted, so perhaps a new partner was the only answer for them.

For couples who truly want to succeed, staying away from nitpicking, bullying, and blaming helps tremendously. Sometimes you may not think you are engaging in these behaviors; take a step back and look at your list. You see the issue, you talk about the issue using "I" language and constructive criticism, and you move toward the middle. You let the issue go and you don't bring it up again or keep a tally or "laundry list." Healthy relationships cannot tolerate laundry list arguments. You don't need to keep a balance sheet so that you and your partner know who did what when. Your eyes should be focused on the present and the future. Past issues have been addressed and need no further mention. Usually one person has a better memory and the other flounders. That doesn't mean the partner with the better memory is a "better mate" and that yardstick should not be used. Let arguments and issues go. Don't keep bringing them up. That balance and a commitment to that balance will keep love strong and help a relationship last.

Bigger Items for Compromise

Many issues can come up when couples run aground, such as where to live, visiting with family, children, money, sex, and a host of other items that can't be settled simply by saying, "Okay, I'll empty the dishwasher if you walk the dog."

The bottom line for happy coupling is two healthy people who care for themselves and for their relationship. The words of the day, every day, should be trust, love, and compromise. Sometimes one person will be benefiting much more than the other, but it is assumed each will take turns at helping their mate fulfill their dreams and being the healthiest person they can be. If your partner goes to school or meetings or is involved with different organizations, it helps if you support their work and hobbies; a fulfilled person comes back to the relationship with a warm and cheery glow. At least they *should* come back that way. No matter what, each person should pursue interests outside the relationship and come back to the relationship happier and whole.

Compassion

A common denominator among healthy, loving couples is that each partner has compassion for the other. In action, compassion is taking care of each other. "Taking care" means thinking about how you speak to each other, being careful to not call each other names, get nasty, or fight dirty. Healthy couples have arguments and discussions but it's not about playing head games or winning. It's about what is best for the relationship. If one person is always winning, chances are the relationship is losing.

To come to resolution, each partner must show some restraint, usually verbal or emotional. Many couples get into a pattern of arguing that may or may not be good for the relationship. If you storm out and that causes your partner to feel abandoned, ignored, and unloved, then you're not fighting fair. If you're calling your partner names, jumping to conclusions, or undermining your partner's good feelings for no productive reason, you're not fighting fair. And if you're not fighting fair, then you're not bringing care and compassion to the relationship.

Arguments and disagreements are about working through conflict to make things better and life easier. It is not about going in circles or trying to one-up your partner with logical twists and turns. If you get a perverse pleasure out of decimating your partner in an argument to prove that no one can win with you, it shows you care more about your reputation as a word warrior than about your partner's well-being. If you care more about your skill in figuratively cutting someone off at the knees, you are probably upsetting someone beyond what is right and reasonable. To be a compassionate partner, you have to care more about the health of the relationship and the satisfaction of both of you than winning an argument. If one person is winning, everyone is losing.

Another way to have compassion is to sincerely care about the challenges your partner may face at work, with family, with friends, with physical and emotional health. Asking your partner, "How are you doing?" with a tone of true caring can make someone feel truly loved especially if going through an individual crisis or problem. A client whose department was facing layoffs came home every night exhausted from the stress. One day her boss told her she was valued and would not be on the layoff list. Her partner said, "Isn't that great news?" She said she felt guilty watching her co-workers pack their things and her workload had increased while salaries would remain stagnant. Her partner did not see her point of view and kept insisting she needed to be more positive. Although it's hard to imagine being down when your boss tells you that you will not be losing your job, if your partner is upset, try to show compassion first and then gently suggest the positive side of things. When you're not facing the same challenge, issue, loss, or difficulty as your partner, showing compassion first is usually the best idea.

Communication, Compromise, and Compassion: Examples

Example 1: A man reported that his soon to be ex-wife was too lenient with the children when it came to his belongings. She routinely allowed the older boys to take hammers and screwdrivers out of his toolbox. He asked her many times to guard his tools when he was not home, but her refrain was that they weren't going to destroy the tools. But then they lost them. When he put a lock on the toolbox, the boys found other things to use as hammers. Finally he locked the garage altogether and only he had a key and a door opener. His wife was upset but unwilling to set a boundary that the boys not borrow his things. The disagreement broadened when the boys did not respect other boundaries they were given, and the younger girls started taking things from the bathroom or using all the shampoo or toothpaste. The lack of boundaries, which did not crop up until the children were older, started as a broken shoelace issue that divided them. Had the husband and wife stood united against the children's boundary crashing and come to a solution, such as getting the boys their own tools, the couple may have averted divorce. The husband said, "It didn't seem like we had a lot of problems, but the ones we did have made me crazy. I never felt safe in my own house with my own children as my wife looked the other way when they did exactly what I didn't want them to do." Additionally, the children never did the chores he assigned to them, and they faced no consequences from their mother. "They never finished their chores; in fact, they barely began them and my wife said nothing, leaving me to be the bad guy when I got home."

Many couples argue over child rearing. If these kinds of issues aren't worked out before children arrive (and many can't be foreseen), it may be time to seek counseling, take a parenting class, or agree on concepts such as personal space and responsibility, logical consequences (as explained in *GPYB*), and healthy boundaries to ensure that a family remains intact. In a healthy family, everyone feels safe, that their belongings are their own and will be there the next time they want to use them. Everyone in the family should have good boundaries and expect them to be respected. A healthy atmosphere of compromise and compassion should exist.

Example 2: The parents described in the preceding example failed to present a united front. This is a major pitfall of parenting. Tell Johnny that bedtime is 9:00 PM, whether he likes it or not. Mom may think he's entitled to stay up until 9:30, but Dad is adamant that Johnny get his sleep. They may compromise on 9:15, but in many cases, the compromise is not that simple.

One woman reported that her husband, a well-known attorney, wanted their kids to take all honors courses, beginning in middle school. He was a "tiger" dad. She had a college degree but thought children in honors courses spent too much time on homework. Her mistake was saying this in front of the children. One day she yelled at her husband, "Not everyone wants to spend their entire life behind a door reading big, clunky books!" The children heard this and, one by one, began to drift off their studies, telling Dad that they weren't sure they were really honor students and they spent too much time on homework.

It's important to talk about parenting styles away from the children. Some parents want to be their child's friend, often to the detriment of the other parent. They may whisper, "Well, I want you to be able to stay up late, but you know how [Dad/ Mom] is." This is not healthy for you or your child. As I explain in *GPYB*, it is important to be a parent and not a friend to your children. They need the security that comes from knowing you are in charge. It is also important for your children to know they have two parents who care enough to be united in their upbringing.

Perhaps you and your partner need to visit school and talk to your children's teachers before making decisions about their educational needs. Additionally, perhaps each child has a different goal. Taking that into consideration is important. Even at a very young age, some children are gifted, some are average, and some need extra help. It's important, as parents, to recognize the difference. When you talk things out to meet in the middle, you put communication, compromise, and compassion to work for you and the whole family.

Example 3: One woman said, "My husband is very messy so we have a housekeeper, but he pays all the bills and chauffeurs the children around to their various after-school activities. He maintains the cars, puts the garbage out, and deals with landscaping and snow removal. He also picks at food while I'm cooking, leaves his clothes on the floor, wet towels on the bed, and uses good linens for cleaning up the garage. If I could get him to stop using the linens and leaving the wet towels on the bed, I could live with everything else." Consequently she hides the good towels and checks the bed as soon as he comes out of the shower, reminding him put the towel in the laundry. He finds her too fussy about the house and doesn't see the big deal about using good towels to wipe off grease. He shrugs, "Just wipe off the grease and buy more linens." When asked what she does that irritates him he says, "She's on the computer all the time, she hangs everything up, she moves furniture about once a month, and puts things where I can't find them." Her good qualities include grocery shopping, cooking, and doing the dishes. "As long as she does those three things, I'm fine with everything else." They each take responsibility for their part in the relationship, including what to accept or change. Early on they had discussions about important matters and found they were mutually compatible in most areas, including core values and their view of life. They worked out what may have been problematic. Overall, they understand their responsibilities to themselves, to the house and kids, and to each other. Although they each flash some anger over minor issues that come up repeatedly, they accept each other's flaws and shortcomings, communicate the best they can, find some compassion for the other, and try to compromise in the middle.

Any couple that truly wants to succeed has to stay in "accept or change" mode, where leaving is not an option. If something is no more than it appears to be (the issue is about wet towels on the bed, not about power and control), then it's a matter of accepting it or changing it. In any fair negotiation, people want something "coming back" before they just accept it. For example, they want to know that their partner is willing to put another item on the table before relinquishing the right to do or not do something. Healthy partners learn to compromise and bargain. Healthy partners teach their children the same thing, and everyone thrives in a healthy household.

Example 4: A couple argues every day about bed making. The husband, having spent years in the military, wants it made with the sheets pulled tightly and corners tucked. The wife couldn't care less about the bed and feels fine just pulling the comforter up over it. They argue about this all the time. What is the solution? (1) Find out if the bed is really what they are arguing about and (2) find out why. Perhaps the fight is not about the details of bed making but rather the broader issue that the husband wants power and control and the wife does not feel she can win against him and employs passive-aggressive methods to undermine what he wants. Passive-aggressiveness is an indirect resistance to avoid confrontation, and when it is present, there are usually demands or expectations on the other side of it. Looking at other patterns in this couple's life may indicate if that dynamic is at play or if it's truly just about making the bed.

A question for them is, How important is this? The husband may have had a series of partners who refused to comply with his demand to make the bed "properly." Is there something in the life inventory that may give a clue about this? Sometimes the issue your partner is having is not with you but with someone else. Those partners may have meant less than his wife does now. However, he grew to insist that the bed be made because that was a small thing in comparison to everything else in other relationships. But his wife has been a good partner and mate and is much more thoughtful and caring than anyone before, which is why he married her. Therefore, he needs to take a step back and weigh the importance of bed making against what his wife means to him. If he's able to do that, he may find that his wife is more important and on the days he leaves for work first, he needs to get used to the bed not being made the way he would like. If her husband takes that important step forward, the wife should reciprocate with being a bit more thoughtful about how she makes the bed. This is how repetitive arguments end, compromise and compassion begin.

chapter 10

Real Love Is
As Real Love Does

There is fun, fireworks, and fantasies, and then there is real love and real life. This chapter is about the latter. Discussing what real relationships between real people are like sounds boring to many people who are looking for the magic bullet to finding true love. This book is not an infomercial and the techniques described in it take effort. However, if you put in the effort up front, you will reap the rewards, as your effort not only becomes second nature but fun as well. Yes, effort can equal fun! The effort involved in making a true and loving relationship last comes up front. When you both know how to use a healthy communication style and loving techniques, you will glide along as two healthy and happy people.

When I ask people why they want a partner, they usually say "to share my life with" or "to grow old with" or "to lean on when times are tough." Healthy people know that a good relationship should be both a springboard to a well-rounded, enjoyable life and a refuge from the storm known as "life you didn't count on happening." It should be the place that rocks when times are good and functions as your rock when times are bad. How do you make that happen?

The Good News: How to Make It Rock!

The most successful couples have a few things in common:

1. They both work for the good of the relationship.
2. They have prenegotiated tasks and responsibilities.
3. They each have outside interests and hobbies.
4. They keep an attitude of gratitude for what they have and don't sweat the small stuff.
5. They choose their battles.
6. They incorporate a lot of play into their interactions and have a sense of humor even when things go wrong.
7. They learn from each other and help balance each other where styles are concerned (parenting, house-keeping, spending habits). They aim for the middle.
8. They communicate, compromise, and care for each other.
9. They look at life from a shared perspective.

10. They each work to ensure that their relationship makes both their lives fuller and richer.

We're Having a Party

Your relationship is like a party: there are preparations to make before and cleanup to do after. However, no matter how well prepared you are and how much you look forward to the party, things sometimes go wrong. It can be something benign such as putting too much salt in the potato salad or something comical such as the dog running through the flowers. It can be frustrating when you turn on the sprinkler to fill the kiddie pool and it's broken or Aunt Elsie didn't show and she was in charge of the drinks or the shed door is pulled off by a well-meaning brute of a cousin looking for something to fix the sprinkler faucet. But it can start to get ugly if the dog gets tangled in the tablecloth and all the food comes crashing down or a child falls and needs to go to the hospital or someone with allergies is stung by a bee.

No matter what, you attend to what needs attending to, let go of what doesn't, improvise as necessary, and work as a team that knows how to roll with the punches. At the end of the day you don't bark at each other and blame "your" cousin, "your" aunt, the faucet problem I told you about weeks ago, the dog being loose when one person wanted him leashed during the party, or how no one thought of buying extra food or drinks in case something happened to the food you had or the drinks you didn't.

In life, things happen under all conditions. If you're throwing a party, you hope for a good turnout, nice weather, and nothing unexpected, but stuff happens. If you're preparing for a hurricane, you nervously try to decide whether to stay or evacuate. You decide to evacuate and while the rains are pounding and the winds are howling, you're nervous about your house. But at the shelter you meet new friends and later find a family member stopped by to see how your house was and you never knew this person cared. Between the parties that go wrong and the hurricanes that go right, you find shadows in the sunlight as well as silver linings in the clouds. Mature, healthy people don't find someone to blame for a misfortune and know enough to be grateful when scary things turn out okay.

Terrible, horrible things happen to the best of us and the worst of us. It's not a matter of having someone shield us from it, but rather having someone there with us helping us through the storm or the party gone wrong. It's about not bailing on your partner or assigning blame for whatever is going wrong. If you don't think anyone would blame a partner for a hurricane, you are mistaken. There are people who find something, anything, to say when facing a storm, a tornado, or an earthquake about what precautions their mate forgot to take. That is not how good relationships work. Instead, you hold on to each other, count blessings and heads, and keep yours down. We all like to simply pop off from time to time to people who will just take it, but that is not good for them or good for us. We must always care enough to take care of our most precious assets: each other.

When things are going well, enjoy it and bask in it. Take time, each day, to be grateful for what you have and try to have fun with each other even after the end of a long day. Take some time, when there are no parties or hurricanes, to enjoy each other and try to think of a way to keep fun in your life. Whether it's a date night or a lunch together or just sitting and listening, really listening, to each other, take the time when things are quiet to bask in it together. Having a party, even a quiet party, is important for every couple.

Remember When You Made Each Other Laugh?

A couple came to see me who had been high school sweethearts. They parted for a short time and then reconnected in their early twenties. After their dalliances with others, they decided that they never cared so much as they did for each other. They spent much time together as teenagers and believed they knew each other well. When the man called the woman to reconnect and confessed that he didn't think he would find another like her, he said, "This is a corny analogy, but it's like a birthday cake for Jeff. You call the bakery and order a cake with the inscription Happy Birthday Jeff! and no one ever picks it up. Sure there are other Jeffs in the world but what are the chances that someone is going to call that bakery for a birthday cake for Jeff before that one goes bad?" The woman confessed she had no idea what he was saying. He said, "My love for you is like a birthday cake for Jeff. It's not good for anyone else. And if you don't come and get it, it will grow moldy and stale." She burst out laughing, as did he. She said, "It seemed like a strange reason to get serious with your high school sweetheart, but I smiled every time I thought about it and remembered how much I liked him."

Over the years they bought houses, some with big problems, had children, one with a disability, and were in a near-fatal car accident that drove them apart instead of bringing them together. When I saw them, they appeared to be on the brink of divorce with many wedges between them. We went through some of their history the first few visits and they argued about a lot of the same recollections, each accusing the other of getting it wrong.

When we revisited their post–high school reconciliation story, the "birthday cake for Jeff" story came out. Both started to laugh in what had been a serious session until that point. When we got past the brink of divorce and started to construct their couples list, both immediately wanted to include "birthday cake for Jeff" on it. It was a big picture item, a silly relic from long ago, but it made them both smile and remember why they were together.

Every couple has a silly story from when they first met or first became involved. Anything that reminds you of that should be on the couples list. In the pre–cell phone age, one man waited for his soon-to-be wife at the wrong ferry pier while she fretted at the other. Each was distraught that the other had walked off or didn't care, but when they finally figured it out, they were both happy and relieved but a bit angry. To lessen the impact of the episode on their relationship, the man bought a small ceramic ferry and sent his fiancée a card that read, "I will always be the harbor you can dock your ferry in." Again it seemed corny years later, but it made them both smile when recalling it. Try to keep mementos and other items around that make you smile, laugh, or connect in a way you can only do with each other.

Now that you have found someone to love who loves you, there are ways to ensure that love lasts and that you look at arguments, disagreements, boundaries, and faultfinding in an entirely new way. If you live by the dictate that "love is an action" when you set healthy boundaries and you see the big picture—that this is your one precious life and you will not waste it on people who are not worthy or don't see your worth— your perspective on what you need in a partner changes. You lose the desperation that may have been present in other choices. Prior to finding "the one," know you are alone because you are being selective and careful about your next choice. Being alone isn't about feeling desperate enough to latch on to anyone. It's a deliberate choice that reflects your determination to find one who will fit into your ideal of what real love is and how real love works in the real world.

Real Love Involves Both Your Head and Your Heart

Sometimes we need to give up our movie-based notions of romantic love so that we can honestly assess a person. Being led by emotion or choosing someone who can make your heart swoon can be a mistake. Often the catch in the throat you feel has nothing to do with love or compatibility or ability to sustain interest on your part or the other person's part. People never want to hear that. Usually the more starry-eyed they become, the greater the upset later on. You didn't want to hear that, did you? That's okay, neither did I.

Sometimes people confuse romantic love and real love or put them in opposition. They can be the same. The problem is that a host of other things parade as romantic love. Some people get off on the highs and lows of puppy love even though puppy love is not sustainable. Puppy love doesn't stay up with the kid who has a temperature, deice the car, or run for groceries when you have the flu. Puppy love, erotic love, love that sets your heart ablaze and your knees a-knocking typically doesn't last for the long haul. Can real love start as puppy love? Absolutely. However, two people must have deep compatibility for long-term success. Do we sometimes pass up a good match because we're not shaking in our shoes or obsessed with another? Yes. Can I tell you which it is when you meet someone? No.

You can have real love and romantic love without a roller-coaster feeling. True love, real love, "I've found my soul mate" love can be kind and soft. You can be nervous and lose your appetite with real love, but it starts to even out as you become more "real" with each other. When the deep knowledge begins to form and you invite each other into your lives and reveal who you really are, that is when real love forms and takes hold. You eventually stop being nervous and you regain your appetite. And you smile. A lot.

Unconditional Love:
What Does It Really Mean?

There is no phrase so misinterpreted as "unconditional love." People use it as an excuse to stay in bad relationships. They use it as some ideal they chase when they are not even sure what it means. They use it when they say, "I believe in marriage," or "I believe in loving someone until they can love themselves," or "I'm religious and want to love unconditionally," or "I can't say 'if you do this, I'm out' because that is not unconditional love."

Unconditional love means "I love you no matter what happens," not "no matter what you do to me." *It means under any condition.* The original wedding vow ideal is love, honor, and cherish, for richer or poorer, in sickness and in health. "Unconditional love" doesn't mean, "I love you if you hurt me." That is not in any wedding vow imaginable. No one says that on their wedding day (or whenever they decide to commit) and *no one should.* Commitment ends when repetitive hurt comes in. Unconditional love means "I love you, love is an action, and you come first with me." Unconditional love means, "I love you no matter what conditions occur. No matter what changes life throws our way, I will not take it out on you and I will not forget you exist."

If we are healthy, we must set boundaries for people to stay or go in our life. These are standards, and you learned all about them in previous chapters. They don't disappear when you find someone to settle down with.

Many people get upset when a person continues to be the person they met. "But he's so messy!" "But I thought she'd start cooking." "I hate how much he drinks!" "I don't understand her need to stop off with her friends now that we're living together." If those things were present when you met and built a loving relationship, why do you think they would be different now that you've made a commitment and are living together? Accepting someone warts and all means that you knew this going in, so why would you expect it to change? If your partner's behavior is hurting you, such as the guy who drinks to oblivion on the way home every night, why are you getting deeper into the relationship instead of getting out? You can't accept unacceptable behavior, put a ring on it, and then ask it to change. No matter how bad the behavior, if you knew it going in, that's not fair. However, you don't need to let it continue if it's hurting you.

It does not have to rise to the level of abuse. Many couples argue over forgetfulness. Being forgetful is a human imperfection that almost everyone has in varying degrees. It's like leaving the cap off the toothpaste or hanging the toilet roll the opposite way you do. No need to leave or punish someone over it. Don't say, "If you loved me unconditionally, you would put the cap back on the toothpaste." Because the retort to that is, "If you loved me unconditionally, you wouldn't ask me to put the cap back on the toothpaste." Unconditional love does not result in stalemate.

Love, honor, and cherish your partner who loves, honors, and cherishes you. It means treat each other with kindness and dignity while accepting the annoyances, irritations, and the things you're always going to argue about no matter what. Love, honor, and cherish means keeping everything in perspective. It means accepting someone's flaws but allowing healthy debate when possible and compromise on the small things. Go, love, and be loved. As I tell all my readers and clients, "You can do it." The following stories show how.

Epilogue: Love Stories

Maya and Martin

Martin was a first-year law student when he was invited to a party given by Maya's roommate. Maya was having a bad day and decided to hide out in her room.

Martin arrived at the party and, being an inquisitive person, perused the books on the shelf, drawn to the titles he was reading. He began to think to himself, "Who is the person who owns these books? I have to meet her!" As Maya reluctantly came out of her room, her roommate was telling Martin those were Maya's books. Unabashedly, Martin made his way to Maya, introduced himself, and they began to talk. Her books were about many different subjects. As they began to talk, their conversation was so lively and enthralling that a small circle formed around them. That night Maya called her mother and said, "I think I met the man I'm going to marry."

Martin found it difficult to concentrate on anything but Maya, let alone the rigors of law study. Still, he pursued both Maya and his legal education. They married while he was still in law school and had a daughter, Sahel. She was joined by two sisters, Selma and Miel. Martin practiced law in the United States for several years before going to work for his family's company in the Philippines. Maya homeschools the girls and they are well-educated, well-traveled, and very happy. Love happened for them when neither was looking or thinking that it would. It was a matter of being out there, living life, and being open to finding someone who is the best person you're ever going to meet.

Annie and Tony

Annie lived in Cincinnati and Tony lived in Denver, but they met when Tony came to Ohio to visit family and friends. Annie was bracing for the breakup she knew was about to happen and both she and a friend, also on the verge of a breakup, spent the night "whining" (according to Annie) while Tony patiently listened to them. Annie says her life was a mess and she had given her self-image over to her soon-to-be ex boyfriend and his friends. As she predicted, the boyfriend broke up with her and she was a mess. A friend introduced her to my blog before *GPYB* came out. Annie posted some thoughts and became close friends with two other blog readers.

Meanwhile, she set about trying to figure out her life and saw her new friend Tony whenever he came to Ohio, as well as once when she went to visit Denver with another friend. Her self-esteem was rising thanks to affirmations and positive self-talk and she worked up the nerve to tell Tony she liked him. His response was, "I live in Denver."

No longer willing to play the fool, Annie was worrying about her life, and not about Tony. However, her turn back toward her own life put him on notice that she wasn't to be upended by his nonchalant brush-off, and suddenly he was ready to pursue her.

They went back and forth between the two cities, yet Annie was convinced that the long-distance relationship was never going to work. She was about to end things with him when he asked her to marry him. He presented her with an emerald engagement ring, somehow knowing she didn't like diamonds. Annie said yes and they were married this past May. The two blog friends attended and each wrote me afterward, "He's a good one!" so that I would approve. When I spoke with Annie, I asked her about Tony and she replied, "He is the love I didn't know I was looking for." She described her type, which was the complete opposite of Tony and how he lives his life. Her "type" had never worked out for her and she had nothing but heartache in pursuing the men she thought were the ones for her. She says she learned some important lessons: "I was able to use the blog as a space to work through that last breakup and, more importantly, all of the baggage I was carrying. I still tell myself that you can't give up before the miracle happens. Do your work. Keep your side of the street clean. Don't force it. Love is an action. Your partner shouldn't make you cry. The right one shows up. Love doesn't have to hurt. I am a lady of grace and dignity and will not settle for less than I'm worth. All of these things are true. With Tony I have a love I think will last our lifetime." As this book was going to print, Annie and Tony announced that they would be parents in 2015!

Candice and Hank

Candice was perky, personable, sweet, and endearing. In addition to being lovely and kind, Candice was a good friend, a loving daughter and granddaughter, and an avid animal lover.

Unfortunately, like many a kind and affable person, she found herself on the wrong end of unavailable or unemotional men who took advantage of her good nature.

Not only nice but smart, Candice attended the University of Virginia and Vanderbilt University. After working for a few years, Candice decided to return to school and attend a competitive program at Stanford University to learn all she could about becoming a young entrepreneur.

Putting her love life aside, Candice concentrated on her business enterprise and setting up shop in the very competitive New York City world. Ever the smart thinker, she jumped at every opportunity to put herself "out there" to grow her business. Her circles widened as she appeared in magazine articles and on television shows. Doing what *GBOT* suggests, building a life of her own in many different ways, Candice was involved in business, social, community, and philanthropic events.

One night at a fund-raiser, a friend asked if the man standing near them was Hank from UVA. To Candice's surprise, it was. Hank was a success at IBM and was also widening his circles and dedicating himself to community and philanthropic causes. As *GBOT* suggests, look for a partner who looks at life the same way you do. Both Candice and Hank adhered to the saying, "To whom much is given, much is expected." They both felt blessed and rewarded by life and were giving back at young ages.

Even though they had known each other while attending the University of Virginia and reconnected on and off during the next thirteen years, they both had their own lives and became someone in their own right before settling down with someone.

Their meeting in New York was happenstance, but it doesn't happen if you don't put yourself out there in your own life and in your own right.

I didn't meet Hank while they were dating and falling in love. Knowing Candice's history, I was somewhat skeptical of the relationship. I first saw him as he walked out of Oheka Castle onto the lawn to take his place at the altar on his wedding day. He was grinning from ear to ear and I, along with the other guests, laughed as Hank came strolling out and I thought, "I approve!"

As Candice walked out, he looked at her as only a love-struck man can. They wrote beautiful vows, and I was convinced they were destined for each other: no one would love Candice more than he. When they returned from a honeymoon in Europe, we spoke and I asked her to describe her missteps with men prior to Hank and she said, "The journey to greatness begins with a small step (and sometimes in the wrong direction)." You can make mistakes in relationships—so long as you right your ship and learn what you need to learn, you will be fine! Candice learned from her mistakes and stepped back and built her own life. While concentrating on that, she reconnected with Hank, who had also been building his own life. Together, they are a wonderful and beautifully paired couple.

Phil and Jared

Phil was a flight attendant based in Chicago who had broken up a long-distance relationship with someone in San Francisco.

He would have liked to move to San Francisco, but the housing market made that impossible because his house was worth less than he owed on it, so that he couldn't sell it. Angry because he had no control over the housing market, he was convinced that he would never get over his relationship or find someone better.

We spoke about two years later and he had just met Jared, a Chicago native. Jared was unsure if he was ready even though years had passed since his previous relationship ended. It took them awhile to become exclusive as Phil wanted to be sure that he was over his own previous relationship. The lack of certainty came from remaining in contact. When I told him it was time to go "no contact" with his former partner in San Francisco, he reluctantly agreed. Once he did that, he relaxed with Jared and was able to become exclusive and committed.

When Illinois made gay marriage legal, Phil excitedly called me to say that he and Jared were going to be married. He had finally let go of his last relationship and made the effort to show Jared how much he loved him. Phil said, "I almost lost Jared by staying in touch with someone who had treated me unkind and gave me an ultimatum at a time in my life when I couldn't respond. It's important to look at your partner who loves you and make the commitment rather than pining after someone who didn't take you or your circumstances into consideration. Love is what you do, and also what you don't do. Jared cares about me and makes me feel loved every day and I am showing him the same. When it's equal, it's the best it can ever be."

Janine and Paulie

When I first met Janine, she was a forty-two-year-old single mom with two jobs who lamented that she was never going to meet another man. Her three kids were very active in school sports and activities and she was exhausted most of the time.

Still, she did try to find some "me" time and pursue her own hobbies and interests. One of her interests was photography and a new class was opening up that didn't interfere with work, her children's activities, or any other enterprise she was involved in. She bought a used camera and set out to class very excited to be doing something for herself. At first she struggled and found some of the terminology hard to grasp. "I wanted to give up," she said, "I didn't have a lot of time and what I thought was going to be fun, wasn't." Still, she hung in there since she did find peace on her walks to fulfill some of her assignments. In fact, walking around to find interesting things gave her a lot of serenity and calm that being a single mom did not afford her much of the time.

Because of the walks, she hung in with the class. The second part of the class was learning Adobe Photoshop. Not feeling very confident with computers, she again considered dropping out. In the first few sessions, everyone in the class seemed to get it while she struggled with "layers." She said, "I knew there was no nature walk that was going to make me comfortable with Photoshop so I was ready to throw in the towel." She had barely gotten to know most of her classmates as she did not have time to mingle outside class and usually rushed right home.

One night as she struggled with Photoshop, she put her head on the desk in defeat. The man seated next to her reached over and patted her ever so slightly on the head. She reared back. He seemed startled, "I'm sorry if I was forward, but you just looked like you could use some encouragement." She smiled and shrugged, and he shared that he too was struggling with Photoshop. She moved her chair over to his station and they found that they each understood different things and could help each other.

That was not all. The man was a single dad who struggled with alone time and dating. He was a year older than she and they went for coffee after class a few nights. Eventually they managed to squeeze in a few dates. After six months they introduced the kids and almost two years later, they were married.

Janine says, "It seems like common sense now to put yourself out there, find some alone time, learn something new, and you never know. But if someone had told me that I would meet the love of my life because I hated my photography class, I would have said you were crazy!"

They both continued to learn photography and Photoshop and now take great photos of their kids and family vacations. Paulie says, "I'm glad, for many reasons, that we both stuck it out!"

Susan and Michael

Long before I met Michael, I'd addressed insecurity and fears of abandonment in therapy and support groups. I felt no danger when I met him, and when he said during our first conversation, "I just want to be happy," I shared that feeling and realized that I knew how to be happy on my own. The challenge, for both of us, was going to be, "Can I do this with another person?" We were both veterans of horrifically failed relationships and had managed to figure out a way to be content on our own, tending to our children.

After we started dating, we started acting like school kids instead of the battle-weary relationship veterans we were. I made him a mix tape. He brought me flowers. I cooked for him and gave him a massage. He brought me jewelry and tried to write me a poem. He told me that he had thought he was in love before, but if what we had was love, then, no, he never had been in love before. I felt the same. Yes, we did everything that romantic love entails, but underneath were two solid, knowledgeable people not interested in playing games or being insincere. After meeting Michael, I realized that no one else had ever shown me what could be defined as real love. With some, I saw glimpses of what I thought was love from time to time, but real love is solid, steady, and there every day. Real love exists, as Stephen Levine so aptly puts it, through the "terrible dailyness of life."

Michael and I had strong romantic feelings for each other and acted silly many times, but we had a deep respect and reasoned knowing about our love affair. I couldn't really define a life partner, but I knew one when I met one. I somehow knew that he would be there for me in a way no one else ever was. Was I done playing games with the abandoning crowd? Apparently I was. Was I healed from my relationship with my emotionally unavailable father? Apparently I was. I knew our relationship was authentic. It meant feeling safe and secure while you each set the other's heart ablaze. It's all possible at the same time. Who knew?

Michael and I had a deep friendship, a penchant for having fun together, and a never wavering, unconditional love. Love under all conditions, and trust me when I tell you, life threw everything at us from hard financial times to a child three thousand miles away on life support. We shared the best of times and the worst of times. Through it all we made each other laugh and smile and held each other when we cried. The words "I am there for you" took on a meaning neither of us had ever known.

Some people think the moony feeling of infatuation is love. They love being swept away and "falling in love," even if the person is all wrong. Just because you're into that feeling doesn't make you a romantic and doesn't make that love. You must have some amount of reason in your choices. That swept away feeling doesn't mean it's the one. And not having it doesn't mean it's not. We had different tastes, hobbies, and interests but we supported each other's goals and dreams. He liked to fish and watch NASCAR. I liked to read and tinker with computers. He said books gave him hives but happily joined me at the New York Public Library to work on a school project. I said NASCAR made no sense but bought him tickets, complete with pit pass, several times.

We had standing disagreements, such as the laundry. When I met him, his dining room table was piled high with clean clothes. I was astonished that he quite literally used it as his dresser drawers. When we moved in together, we bought a new bedroom set and he put his clean clothes away. For a while. Then he started to leave them out. First in a basket in the bedroom, then a basket in the kitchen, then in the dryer. I would remind him that he needed to take them out so the rest of us could do our laundry.

I had no intention of doing it for him as I knew I would become resentful if I did. He was the messiest person I've ever known and if someone told me I would ever tolerate such messiness before I met him, I would have said that was not going to happen. I also wasn't going to argue with him about it or try to change him into someone he wasn't. Our compromise was to hire a cleaning lady, and he would clean up his mess before she came in for the weekly cleaning.

After we bought a pool table, he started to leave his clothes on it, and I had visions of the dining table in his bachelor home. When I asked that he remove them, he would shove them into a basket and into a closet. I would open a closet and stare down at the pile of clothes and shake my head. I started to refer to it as the "closet compromise." Most people who knew me could not believe I never said a word about it.

He had similar issues with things I did. He could back a tractor trailer into an alley and couldn't understand that I could not back my small car out of the massive driveway without hitting something. Once, as we were both leaving for work, I backed into his brand-new truck. He got out, looked at the damage, shook his head, and got back into the truck. I wouldn't have blamed him for being angry or bringing it up at some point, but he never did. There were many things we could have argued about, but we each had learned—probably the hard way—that is not the way to have a good relationship.

If someone asked me to name the worst moment of my life, it was when the doctor told me he had three to six months to live. I went deaf and blind for a moment and all I could hear was the screaming of my soul. But then Michael showed me what was important. When we went to his first radiation treatment, he looked at the children and said, "I've lived my life. They should be out playing." He reassured a young mother who was frightened to have surgery. Michael's tumors were too advanced for him to have surgery, but he comforted and encouraged her. Another man spoke no English and Michael made gestures to him that everything would be fine. He thought it unfair for a child or a mother or a man to have cancer treatments without having anyone to speak to in their own language. There was even an inmate from the nearby prison who came in for treatment. The guards kept him on the other side of the waiting room. Everyone ignored him, except Michael. He nodded to him every day and asked how he was. When I asked him why, he said that he was going home with his loving wife to a warm meal and a nice bed, but what did that man have to go back to? For six weeks we made a two-hour trip daily for his treatments, know-ing it wasn't going to make much difference, but I learned to cherish those days with him. When I thought it was unfair that I was losing him, I was grateful to have him for a while.

When Michael took sick, there wasn't anything I wouldn't do for him. When I discovered his first caregiver neglecting him,

I stood behind him in a wheelchair and yelled for her to leave. Michael had stopped walking and had difficulty talking but that sweet man reached up, held my hand, and croaked out to her, "We have each other's back." We certainly did. All the work I did through affirmations, observations, preparation, and putting boundaries and standards in place led me to spending fifteen years with the most wonderful person I've ever known as well as knowing in my darkest hours after he passed that one day I would be okay again. Though brain cancer took that loving man from me, I have known real love and that's the best feeling to know. Real love exists and you can have it in your life if you love and value yourself first. It's worth every ounce of work to be healthy enough to recognize it and accept it into your life.

Bibliography and Recommended Reading

The books listed here, both academic and pop psychology, can be useful to you in dating and developing healthy relationships.

Arylo, Christine. *Choosing Me Before We*. Novato, CA: New World Books, 2009.

Beattie, Melody. *Beyond Codependency*. Center City, MN: Hazelden, 1987.

———. *Codependent No More*. New York: Ballantine, 1986.

———. *The New Codependency*. New York: Simon & Schuster, 2008.

Beck, Aaron. *Love Is Never Enough: How Couples Can Overcome Misunderstandings, Resolve Conflicts, and Solve Relationship Problems*. New York: Harper & Row, 1988.

Black, Claudia. *Double Duty*. New York: Ballantine, 1990.

Bowen, Murray. *Family Therapy in Clinical Practice*. New York: Jason Aaronson, 1978.

Bowlby, John. *Attachment and Loss*. Vol. 1, *Attachment*. New York: Basic, 1968.

———. *Attachment and Loss*. Vol. 2, *Separation: Anxiety and Anger*. London: Penguin, 1973.

———. *Attachment and Loss*. Vol. 3, *Loss, Sadness, and Depression*. London: Penguin, 1973.

——— *Making and Breaking of Affectional Bonds*. London: Routledge, 1979.

———. *A Secure Base*. London: Routledge, 1988.

Campbell, Susan M. *Truth in Dating*. Novato, CA: New World Library, 2004.

Corsini, Raymond J., and Danny Wedding, eds. *Current Psychotherapies*. Stamford, CT: Brooks/Cole Cengage Learning, 2011.

Cowan, Connell, and Melvyn Kinder. *Women Men Love, Women Men Leave*. New York: Crown, 1987.

Elliott, Susan J. *Getting Past Your Breakup: How to Turn a Devastating Loss into the Best Thing That Ever Happened to You.* New York: Da Capo, 2009.

Ellis, Albert. *Feeling Better, Getting Better, Staying Better: Profound Self-Help Therapy for Your Emotions.* Atascadero, CA: Impact 2001.

Estes, Clarissa Pinkola. *Women Who Run with Wolves.* New York: Ballantine, 1992.

Ferguson, Craig. *Does This Need to Be Said? The Full Concert Experience.* DVD. Comedy Central, 2011.

Firestone, Robert, and Joyce Catlett. *Psychological Defenses in Everyday Life.* New York: Human Sciences Press, 1989.

Freud, Sigmund. *The Standard Edition of the Complete Psychological Works of Sigmund Freud.* Ed. James Stachey. London: Hogarth, 1957.

Gottman, John M. *Seven Principles for Making Marriage Work.* New York: Three Rivers, 1999.

Greenberg, Jay R., and Stephen A. Mitchell. *Object Relations in Psychoanalytical Theory.* Cambridge: Harvard University Press, 1983.

Johnson, Sue. *Hold Me Tight.* New York: Hachette, 2008.

Lerner, Harriet Golhor. *Dance of Anger.* New York: Harper & Row, 1985.

———. *Dance of Intimacy.* New York: Harper & Row, 1990.

Harville, Hendrix. *Getting the Love You Want.* New York: Holt, 1988.

———. *Keeping the Love You Find.* New York: Atria, 1992.

Horney, Karen. *Our Inner Conflicts.* New York: Norton, 1945.

Levine, Stephen. *A Gradual Awakening.* New York: Anchor, 1979.

Levine, Stephen, and Ondrea Levine. *Embracing the Beloved.* New York: Anchor, 1996.

Oliver, Mary. *Selected Poems.* Vol. 1. Boston: Beacon, 1992.

———. *Selected Poems.* Vol. 2. Boston: Beacon, 2005.

Peck, Scott. *The Road Less Travelled.* New York: Touchstone, 1998.

Richo, David. *How to Be an Adult in Relationships.* Boston: Shambhala, 2002.

Scaturo, D. J., et al. "The Concept of Codependency and Its Context Within Family Systems Theory." *Family Therapy* 27, no. 2 (2000): 63–70.

Schnarch, David. *Passionate Marriage.* New York: Norton, 2009.

Sills, Judith. *A Fine Romance.* New York: Random House. 1978.

———. *Getting Naked Again.* New York: Hachette, 2010.

Tice, Louis E. *A Better World, a Better You: The Proven Lou Tice "Investment in Excellence" Program.* Upper Saddle River, NJ: Prentice Hall, 1989.

Winnicott, D. W. *The Child, the Family, and the Outside World.* Boston: Addison-Wesley, 1987.

Young, Kevin, ed. *The Art of Losing.* New York: Bloomsbury, 2010.

Index